D0327642

The French Novel Since the War

The French Novel Since the War

Maurice Nadeau

Translated by A. M. Sheridan Smith

METHUEN & CO LTD
11 NEW FETTER LANE LONDON EC4

First published in France in 1963
as *Le Roman Français Depuis la Guerre*

First published in Great Britain in 1967

Printed in Great Britain by
The Camelot Press Ltd, London and Southampton

Acknowledgements

The publishers would like to thank the following for their kind permission to reprint extracts from the books listed below:

Les Editions du Seuil for *Pour un Romanesque Lazaréen* by Jean Cayrol, and for *Le Degré Zéro de l'Écriture* by Roland Barthes

Editions Gallimard for *La Littérature et le Droit à la Mort* by Maurice Blanchot, © Editions Gallimard; *La Littérature Considérée Comme une Tauromachie* by Michel Leiris, © Editions Gallimard 1939; and *Langue Littéraire et Langue Parlée* by Raymond Queneau, © Editions Gallimard

René Julliard Editeur for *À la Recherche d'un Miroir* by Jean Reverzy

Les Editions de Minuit for 'Le Roman Comme Recherche' from *Répertoire I* by Michel Butor

Librairie José Corti for *La Littérature à l'Estomac* by Julien Gracq

Les Lettres Nouvelles for *Présentation des Lettres Nouvelles*

Editions Bernard Grasset for *Jean et Jean-Paul* by Jacques Laurent

John Calder Publishers Ltd for *Tropisms* and *The Age of Suspicion* by Nathalie Sarraute, 1963

Calder & Boyars Ltd for *Towards a New Novel* by Alain Robbe-Grillet, 1965

Rider & Co. (Hutchinson Publishing Group Ltd) for *Literary and Philosophical Essays* by Jean-Paul Sartre

Contents

The Artist and His Time

The Second World War, like that of 1914–18, came as a profound shock to Western society.

To the direct and indirect results of the war correspond other, less apparent changes that had long been taking place in the human mind as well as in the economic and social sphere.

The rise of fascism in Europe, the reaction in France of a liberalism slightly tinged with socialism, the crushing of the Spanish revolution – different aspects of the same crisis – had provided the conditions for a world-wide conflict involving death and destruction on an unprecedented scale.

This war was to go beyond the limits arbitrarily imposed upon it and set in motion a series of unforeseen consequences. When at last we emerged from the nightmare, we realized that certain values that had for some time been held in question were now seen to be well and truly dead. The period of nihilism, awaited and feared for so long, had at last arrived and we were to live through it. Hunger, destruction, reparations, torture, millions of dead, the deliberately perpetuated murder of millions of human beings in the concentration camps or in the cities and which was to culminate in the instantaneous annihilation of the inhabitants of Hiroshima, held up to European man an unrecognizable image of himself. Beliefs, morality, philosophy, metaphysics, the hard-won achievements of the best minds throughout the centuries, had disappeared with so much else. The exaltation of biological or racial instinct, religious and nationalistic fanaticism, blind confidence in God or in destiny were all seen to have had their day. Western man struggled to his feet once more and surveyed the world that lay in ruins around him.

The wounds were soon patched up and the ruins rebuilt.

Science and technology were now free to restore lost wealth and to increase it to a hitherto unknown extent. With the domestication of atomic energy, new horizons were opened up, promising all kinds of wonders. Man, now planning to travel through the cosmos, enjoyed on his own planet an unprecedented standard of living. The nation-state whose conflicts had brought the world in under fifty years to the edge of destruction, found itself replaced by great continental empires that maintained 'peace' and 'order' in their respective spheres of influence.

But confidence did not return. The new, precarious, world-wide balance of power is constantly at the mercy of a slight increase in weight on one or other side of the scales. The conquests of Science and Technology arouse fear rather than enthusiasm: a series of causes and effects, not all of which are under man's control, could put an end to humanity itself, including its thousand million underfed. Everything seems to indicate that the sickness that brought Europe to the verge of suicide has spread rather than disappeared. The old nations have given way to empires that threaten each other with mutual annihilation. It is on these super-states, with their narrow nationalistic outlook and their insane thirst for conquest, that the fate of the world depends. In the face of possible mass suicide, a 'balance of terror' has been established which in itself presents a terrible temptation.

France emerged from war and occupation a second-class power. The realization of diminished status came as a profound shock and led to a compensatory *folie de grandeur* from which the nation is still suffering. Shaken to its social and economic foundations, divided into two rival camps, each regarding the other as 'traitors', France could envisage no better future than an impossible return to the ranks of the great powers. The dream of national renewal, born in the Resistance movement and which seemed at the Liberation to be near realization, had vanished some five or six years later. With the consent of the new managerial class the older generation of leaders returned and the old fabric was patched up. The times seemed to call for 'consolidation'.

Weakened, and in the worst possible conditions, France had to face new problems caused by the awakening of nationalism among the peoples of her African and Asian colonies, who naturally resented the state of political tutelage and economic exploitation imposed on them by weak and divided masters. Instead of following the example of other European nations and cutting its losses, France chose a policy of stubborn conservatism which engaged her in an exhausting series of losses and defeats. More seriously, she compromised the ideals, of which, since 1789, she had been the privileged guardian, employing in unjustifiable wars and in order to preserve an outdated state of affairs methods whose use she had condemned ten or fifteen years before, legalizing torture and placing herself in the eyes of a horrified world outside the ranks of civilized nations. Sapped by bitterness and resentment, and the feeling of powerlessness to which most of her political leaders had succumbed, France allowed her liberal, democratic façade to crumble and left herself to the mercy of military powers only too anxious to exploit the indifference of the civilian population. She gave herself body and soul to an old-world 'sovereign', who acted as the guardian of the entire nation.

More than any other people in the world today the French feel that their fate is not of their own making. They are witnessing the development of an industrial society of a type common to both East and West which satisfies their material needs. But the French feel in no way committed to this form of society. Their democratic ideals, left for too long in the hands of business-minded politicians, have been thrown away like old clothes. The dream of a free and equitable society vanished when confronted with the reality of Eastern Europe. The way to real progress seemed blocked and the future held nothing better than an obsolescent '*Europe des patries*'. Even a bad conscience seems a bygone luxury to the Frenchman of today. He prefers scepticism, mockery, macabre humour. He cherishes the hope, generally unacknowledged, that he may find the courage to embrace the new values of a younger generation, who, quite justly, reproach their fathers with the humiliation into which they were born. In the meantime, he stands helplessly by as history follows its own course, indifferent to the caprices of his Sovereign.

Against this sombre background, the literary and artistic life of the country has been particularly brilliant. Other cities have recently come into prominence, particularly in the United States and in Japan, but Paris has remained one of the principal centres in which new techniques of artistic creation have been developed, where painters, writers and musicians continue to find an atmosphere congenial and stimulating to their work. Today it is no doubt America that sets the fashion, but only after a glance at what Paris is doing. The theory that art and literature (and other 'superstructures') are conditioned by an economic, social and political basis of which they are the reflection, would appear to be disproved.

In literature, and particularly in the novel (but the same is true of all the arts), it is common practice to place widely different products under the same label. What common criteria exist between the novel, often well-written, that one reads in a railway carriage to kill time, and that rare work which we feel could change the whole course of someone's life? These products carry the same label and their makers are both known as novelists. Could it be that these two things are in some way related? Setting aside these two extreme cases, does it not seem that there are different levels in the novel, some being near the surface, others in the depths and the rest occupying a whole range of intermediate levels. Depending on his temperament and education, and on what he expects to get out of a novel, the reader finds, at different levels, a feeling of satisfaction or answers to the problems that preoccupy him. According to this analogy, the surface levels can be seen as 'reflecting' the sky and the clouds, historical events and the states of mind we share with our contemporaries, while others apparently less sensitive to movements at the surface, pursue their own course, ceaselessly eroding the boundaries of man and the world and the complex reality we call life. Without ignoring completely the pleasures to be obtained from more ephemeral works, let us retain the word literature for those which, as

André Gide put it, do not leave the reader in the same state in which they found him.

This distinction will prevent us from falling into the all too easy temptation of making a 'historical survey', into which we can cram a mass of tendencies, movements, forms, generations and styles (and woe betide us if we miss anyone out!). It will help us to discriminate between what is accidental and what is essential and to clear a way through a proliferating mass in which all aesthetics, traditions, innovations and styles are jumbled together. Moreover, it may enable the reader to glimpse, between the lines of this book, a portrait of the novelist (and of the artist) in our time: living in a certain environment, society, period, sensitive to its unique atmosphere, and able to translate into language its peculiar form, colour and movement, but even more concerned that these things should be conveyed through the medium of a personal vision and idiom. It is no vain desire for originality that motivates him, and his raw material is common to all and available to all, but what he extracts from it remains a mystery. He wishes to create something that is not only beautiful and valuable, but something that will itself become part of the mental equipment of his contemporaries, raw material for reflection, knowledge and action. Art passes from man to man by the medium of exceptional individuals who cannot be reduced to the common characteristics of their time. Yet it is in them that their contemporaries see themselves and their time and it is they who contribute to it that extra dimension without which Plato would be considered solely as the spokesman of the slave state and Samuel Beckett as the reflection of a society that has experienced the 'dehumanization' of man at its ultimate point.

The novel, which in our country is now something like five hundred years old and has long been considered as frivolous, has become one of the commonest forms of literary expression. It is used by the most difficult of our artists, even, or rather especially, when what they have to say has very little to do with the form left to us by Stendhal, Balzac, Flaubert and Zola. Let us be grateful for what we have, as we strive to discover what

Sartre, Camus, Nimier and Robbe-Grillet have brought to us in this noisy and confused post-war period, when a molehill can be taken for a mountain and vice versa. Let us take a close look at our own time and avoid the temptation to step back. Let us risk making mistakes.

1 *The Development of the Novel*

The golden age of the novel is the nineteenth century, with its giants Balzac, Tolstoy and Dickens, authors of immense works, each a complete, carefully constructed world in itself. It was from them that the novel received its letters patent of nobility. In giving the form new rules and conventions, Balzac, Tolstoy and Dickens tried to express the underground workings, the hidden mainsprings of a social and human reality, in which the mysteries of the human mind echo the mysteries of social mechanisms. Their concern was to penetrate these mysteries, to reduce them to a kind of moving inventory, to embody in 'types' the life of certain milieus, classes and individuals. Like God, omniscient and ubiquitous, the novelist created a world which was an exact, comprehensible and significant equivalent of the world around him. It was he who pulled the strings of his *Comédie Humaine*. He claimed 'to compete with the *état civil*'. He was complete master of his instrument: his pen illuminated, probed, revealed.

The immediate successors of these demiurges tried to make of the novel a more exact instrument for conveying information and knowledge, to create a truer image of reality. Not content with being simply an artist, the novelist now had to become a scientist, substituting for his imagination and intuition a knowledge of facts. His chosen field of research was the human heart. But it was not enough that he should be a psychologist; he had also to become a historian, a sociologist, and avail himself of the discoveries of the natural sciences, medicine, law and a knowledge of trades and professions. In declaring themselves to be first 'realists', then 'naturalists', Maupassant, the brothers Goncourt and Zola claimed to adhere strictly to reality and nature. Their predecessors, they believed, had failed to get the truth, still alive and breathing, on to the page. It was enough to speak the truth or to show it, if necessary in its most ordinary, vulgar and sordid aspects, for a veil to be lifted on man and his knowledge of the world.

They wished to follow the example of Flaubert, whose friends and disciples they were, and whom they admired as much for his conscientious artistry as for his concern for truthful and detailed documentation. Flaubert, it is true, worked as a historian and sociologist in *L'Education Sentimentale*,* an archaeologist in *Salammbô*, a philosopher in *La Tentation de Saint Antoine*, and *Madame Bovary* claimed to be a picture of provincial life. They were less affected by the phrase '*Madame Bovary, c'est moi*', which they refused to take seriously, or by Flaubert's dream of writing a novel that would be held together by the internal strength of style alone. As a champion of 'art for art's sake' Flaubert stands at the point at which the novel diverges, discovering a capacity not only for reproducing reality in a living and truthful way, but also for autonomous artistic creation. For Flaubert, art, while revealing a truth outside himself, works upon the truth of his own being. The novel is not so much 'a mirror that one carries with one along a road' as an optical lens that recomposes the rays that pass through it into unexpected images, as in *Bouvard et Pécuchet*.

Flaubert continues to describe 'types', like Emma and Charles Bovary and Félicité, the servant, and 'characters', like Frédéric Moreau, but his two eccentrics, who retire to the country in search of encyclopaedic knowledge, while recognizing the vanity of their aim, are a criticism of a whole period, of certain ambitions attributed to the novel, and are both projections of the author himself. They already live outside any social milieu, like Huysmans' Des Esseintes and the creations of Villiers de l'Isle-Adam, characters who are eccentric to the point of madness, and who seem to have sprung ready-armed from the brain of Dostoyevsky, thousands of miles from Croisset and Paris. While Zola painstakingly narrates 'the natural and social history of a family under the Second Empire' with a visionary talent that fortunately makes one forget his scientific pretensions, the novel swells with

* *Wherever possible, English titles and publishers of French works mentioned in this book have been given in the list of English translations on page 195.*

a reality of its own which the author himself occupies to an increasing degree. Rather than turning himself into a sort of clerk or registrar or a scientist (an amateur scientist at that), he tends to express in the novel the very thing that lay outside the aspirations of the disciples of science: the unity and uniqueness of a particular, living human being. The object thus created is all the more precious in that the novelist pours himself into it entirely, work and author tending to merge into a single, living complex.

Because they failed to understand this, the 'naturalists' left no direct heirs and their place was taken by poets who, since Baudelaire, Rimbaud and Lautréamont, saw literature as fulfilling quite different needs and possessing quite different possibilities. They were less interested in showing, describing, expressing, explaining than in capturing the inexpressible, 'recording a sense of vertigo', establishing secret correspondences between the work of art and the world, giving voice to silence or life to inanity. The close of the century finds Zola exploiting a formula and Mallarmé devoting his whole life to a pursuit of the impossible. Poetry has taken over from the novel as a means of artistic creation.

The young, aspiring writers and artists of the beginning of this century, André Gide, Paul Valéry, Paul Claudel, are more impressed by the explorations of Mallarmé than by the fame, then at its height, of Anatole France, Paul Bourget and Pierre Loti. They reject the novel as an art form and wish to be poets. In his manifesto *L'Esprit Nouveau*, in which Apollinaire defines the new 'modernity', poets, painters and musicians are called upon to form the sacred 'Phalanx' – there is never any mention of novelists. After the 1914–18 war, the novel again comes under fire, this time from André Breton and the surrealists, who find it guilty of exploiting the '*moments nuls*' of a life, when it should be 'changing' them. And if, about this time, André Gide, who exercised a semi-dictatorship over the *Nouvelle Revue Française*, refused the first work by Marcel Proust, it is not because he misjudged the man, as he claimed, but because he misunderstood the artist: he found it inconceivable that a novelist should have the same standards as himself. When he accepted *Jean Barois*, by a young man who was to become a life-long friend, Roger Martin du Gard, Gide remarked that the author was 'no doubt a good fellow, but in no way an artist'.

The discredit into which the novel had fallen lasted until about 1930, in spite of what Marcel Proust had done with the form and in spite of the use made of it by new and vigorous talents. Colette, Mauriac, Duhamel, to a lesser degree Montherlant and Giraudoux, took over the form much as they had found it. They depicted passions, milieus, families, small enclosed communities, particularly in the provinces, with talent, knowledge, audacity, sometimes with fantasy. They did not concern themselves with the questions that beset man in that first post-war period, or appear to have noticed that the world had changed. They possessed neither Martin du Gard's metaphysical anxiety, nor Proust's desire to bend the form to his own ends. Because they believed in the permanence of man and of the world and society in which they lived, they were limited to producing works, often brilliantly written, which seemed more and more dated as the years passed.

But at least they broke with the 'impassibility of the novelist' that constituted the first act of faith of the 'realists', and with their historical, scientific and sociological pretensions. They wished to make their own voices heard and they succeeded, creating atmospheres where there were only lists and descriptions, substituting for demonstration the unexpected effects caused by unusual 'psychologies'. Not so much architects as painters, they created colourful, sensuous compositions, full of finesse and intelligence, and even of poetry and humour.

An impassable barrier separates these upper-class humanists, all confident technicians of the novel, from the anxious, impatient banner-waving young men who were beginning to write about 1930. For them, the novel was less an end in itself than a means of transmitting their ideas in a more acceptable and assimilable form. They took up the novel because it was a form that appealed to the senses, the emotions, the imagination, that was capable of reaching and moving a wider public and could act as a framework and a sounding board for what they had to say. Without wishing to, often without being aware of what they were doing, they knocked down the last props that supported the magnificent 'realist' scaffolding.

By 1930 the post-war world was still unstable. A financial crisis in the United States made itself felt in Europe: millions of unemployed walked the streets of its industrial towns. Fascism on the Mussolini model reached Germany, which swarmed with strange theories about blood, race and the soil. There was talk of a revival of German military revanchism. At first, none of this was taken very seriously, but it soon gave rise to anxiety. The future looked uncertain.

For Gide and Valéry, Duhamel and Mauriac, the 1914–18 war had been a terrible accident, but it had not led them to question the fundamental values on which French society had been built. The Soviets, of course, had quite different values, but they were learning to be sensible; in any case, they were a long way away, and this very fact gained them a certain amount of sympathy. The savage face of Hitlerism, with its threats, its absolute negation of all values, except the oldest and most primitive ones, created a quite different situation. By trying to restore the humanist foundations that the Great War had largely destroyed, French society suddenly found itself powerless before events it did not understand.

The newcomers – Malraux, Giono, Bernanos, Céline, Saint-Exupéry, Queneau and others – were not concerned about the existence of 'unconditional freedom of thought' or whether it was possible to believe in a 'human nature' that was valid for all times and places. Each in his own way presents an image of an unstable, chaotic world in the grip of passion and unreason. Under different forms, and without believing that all is lost, they all ask the same question: what can an individual, thrown into this tragic and incoherent universe, do? What plank can he hold on to to save himself from drowning? Their answers are various and contradictory, as is only to be expected. But they almost all involve a transcending by man of his condition. Their models are the saint, the man of action making history, the Virgilian peasant, the aviator triumphing over the elements and the imperfections of his machine, the anarchist in search (despite the author) of a peaceful and humane world, the cynical, disillusioned philosopher. In each case, the writer is concerned with serious, carefully formulated moral attitudes which engage the whole individual.

Instead of imitating their predecessors, these new novelists adapted the novel to their own ends: one chose the neutrality of reportage, another the sermon, a third thinly-veiled autobiography, active participation in the public events of the time, or a reflection of them in terms of images. They abandoned the notion of a single reality, a single world or a single way of looking at them. All the resources of language are used to a practical end. They strive, with every means at their disposal, to affect the feelings and the imagination, to persuade and to convince. The reality they wish to communicate is essentially subjective. Man, the author, the hero, the narrator are often one and the same person. The reader is always in contact with a 'living' man.

After the defeat of the Spanish revolution, the hope of affecting events, of mastering fate, is dissipated, and if Malraux gave the title of *L'Espoir* to the novel he wrote about his latest experiences it was rather in order to rally those who *despaired* of stopping the course of a world that had gone off the rails. The whole of Western society began to prepare for a war to defend causes in which it hardly believed and which were a disguise either for aggressive instincts that had long lain dormant or for an obstinate desire to arrest social development.

Men caught up in the march of events are in no state to listen to exhortations and prophecies; words lose their effectiveness; writing is regarded as a useless, superfluous activity. Nevertheless, a young writer published *La Nausée* and it caused a sensation. Michel Leiris brought out his *L'Age d'Homme* and long after hostilities had broken out, with France defeated and divided, a young journalist from Algiers, Albert Camus, published *L'Etranger*.

There may not be a rigorous parallel between public events and fiction, but it is curious to notice the extent to which the questions and answers formulated by novelists correspond to those of their contemporaries. The time of moral attitudes is passed (or has not yet returned), and it is in the name of the solitary individual, at the level of his biological, physiological and mythical reactions, that Sartre, Camus and Leiris speak. With them, we are beyond hope and despair, moral values, attitudes to life. Roquentin's nausea expresses the radical refusal to live in a world inhabited by *salauds* (swine); *l'étranger* (the outsider) does not care whether he lives or dies; defying all intellectual and moral censorship, the individual, Michel Leiris, strips himself bare.

At the same time, the fictional element in the novel is reduced to a minimum. It is present as the transparent garment of a philosophy, a metaphysic or a demythologized complex. With the new rules that Sartre elaborated for the novel, a new break was being prepared.

Apart from *L'Etranger*, no new novel reached a wide public during the occupation; the novelist was replaced by the pamphleteer and the poet. The new works by Céline, Giono, Montherlant and Mauriac received only a very limited response. Others remained silent (like Malraux) or chose exile (like Bernanos). Those who spoke up, like Drieu la Rochelle or Robert Brasillach, seemed to have been struck with impotence or mysteriously cut off from reality. The esoteric novels of Maurice Blanchot (*Thomas l'Obscur, Aminadab*), the nostalgic novel of Louis Guilloux (*Le Pain des Rêves*) or the intemporal one of Raymond Queneau (*Pierrot, Mon Ami*) seemed to attract the French reader of either zone less than did the great classics of his own language – Balzac, Stendhal, Proust. He obtained English and American novels on the 'black market'; he discovered Kafka. Novelists and public were coming to a new understanding. But the crushing weight of the occupation had to be lifted first.

2 *The War Dead*

The Second World War was responsible for the deaths of fewer writers than its predecessors, but among these were three excellent novelists: Paul Nizan, Jean Prévost and Antoine de Saint-Exupéry. They were all approaching or had just passed forty. Their work was far from completed.

Paul Nizan

Paul Nizan, who was killed in the battle of Dunkirk in 1940, was a fellow student of Jean-Paul Sartre at the Ecole Normale Supérieure and had remained a close friend despite a divergence in their philosophical and political views.

After *Aden Arabie*, which expresses in the form of a pamphlet a young intellectual's revolt against the state of things existing in France about 1930, Nizan joined the Communist Party. His novels generally depict either a petit-bourgeois world (*Antoine Bloyé*, 1933) or that of young bourgeois intellectuals in revolt against their narrow-minded milieu and the petty lives the future has in store for them. Their revolt is a dead-end and leads them on into adventures in which the police have the upper hand (*La Conspiration*, 1938).

Like most of the novelists of his generation, Nizan made few innovations to the novel on the technical plane and was concerned more with content than with form. His work is assured, intelligent and fluent. Despite the political choice, the 'commitment' he advocated and his own political activity, he was more interested in the problems of his own irresolute, restless and passionate generation, with its changeable opinions, than in discovering a new faith. He described his contemporaries with courage and lucidity, and this brought him a certain prestige among communist intellectuals.

In 1939, at the signature of the Nazi-Soviet Pact, he broke with the Party. He was then subjected to a campaign of insult and calumny at the hands of his former communist comrades that even his death did not bring to an end. In a preface to a new edition of *Aden Arabie*, 1960, Sartre praised his work and paid homage to his friend.

Jean Prévost

Jean Prévost was killed while serving in the maquis of Vercors just before the liberation.

He wrote his first novels and essays at his desk in the Ecole Normale Supérieure. *Dix-Huitième Année* describes the uncertainty of the young intellectuals of the thirties and their apprenticeship to a life which they can see will not be particularly brilliant. But at least, Prévost believes, they ought to view it with lucidity and intelligence and be guided by an ethical system whose values would be entirely non-religious.

Prévost was a moralist, but he was also a critic (*Vie de Montaigne*, 1926; *Les Epicuriens Français*, 1931; *La Création chez Stendhal*, 1942) and an essayist (*Plaisir des Sports*, 1925), as well as a novelist. In *Les Frères Bouquinquant*, 1931, *Rachel*, 1932, *Le Sel sur la Plaie*, 1934, he advocates an everyday heroism whose model he finds among the poor and simple. Intelligent, brilliant, sensitive, with a number of strings to his bow, he never raises his voice and is content to breathe new life into the traditional humanist values he inherited from his master, Alain. His works are lacking in a certain panache and stamina, but they have survived the passage of time fairly well – especially his criticism. A posthumous *Baudelaire*, 1952, confirms the talent of an analyst who was also a fine connoisseur of poetry, as is to be seen in his incomparable translations (*L'Amateur de Poèmes*).

Opposed to all forms of mysticism and mistrustful of the imagination, Jean Prévost showed that a 'radical-socialist'*

* *The term is derived from the name of the* French Radical Party, *sometimes known as the* Radical-Socialist party. *In its origins and underlying philosophy it has something in common with the* British Liberal Party. (*Translator's note.*)

philosophy (the expression is Sartre's) could provide sufficient reason to live or die. He remains our contemporary at least in the sense that, throughout a prolific and varied literary career, he never considered his work to be gratuitous or 'useless'.

Antoine de Saint-Exupéry

The first work by this civil-aviation pilot, *Courrier Sud*, 1928, was noticed by André Gide, who wrote the Preface to his second book, *Vol de Nuit*. On 31st July 1944, his plane crashed into the sea near Corsica: it was his ninth mission as a war pilot. By the time of his death, he had gained a considerable reputation as a writer and moralist with his *Terre des Hommes*, 1939, and *Pilote de Guerre* (published in America in 1942). His work continues to win new admirers, particularly among the young, who now read him more than any other modern writer, even Camus, Sartre or Malraux. His reputation was finally crowned in 1948, at a time when his name was becoming legendary, with the posthumous publication of *Citadelle*, a work more poetic in form than fictional and in which he expounded his own highly personal philosophy and metaphysic. The youth of today finds in Saint-Exupéry a hero after its own heart: a master of language and a master of his own life. It was a life in which, in the practice of his vocation as a pilot, in peace, in the Spanish Civil War and in the war against Hitler, he experienced all the torments of his century.

Saint-Exupéry's first novels are written in the form of reportages on the dangerous, but unromantic life of a civil-aviation pilot, a life in which, constantly confronted with himself, he must call upon his own deepest resources if he is not to lose face in his own eyes. His 'honour' consists in the practice of quite ordinary, but essential qualities, such as tenacity, courage and optimism. 'Doing what a beast is not capable of doing' means not giving up hope in the middle of the desert while waiting for a reserve that may never come; it means believing that man is greater than his absurd destiny and capable of directing not only the blind march of events but the course of his own instincts. The plane is no more than a machine, the desert an unending stretch of sand and his cargo a mere pretext. But it is with these materials that man, doing his job, can construct a life that is otherwise without object or meaning.

In *Terre des Hommes* new preoccupations appear. Saint-Exupéry posits the idea of a fraternity that would bring together all men of goodwill to resist the rise of a barbarism that was ravaging Spain and would soon engulf the whole of Europe. He pleads for a dignity that could be conferred upon no one, but which each man must make claim to and construct for himself. Despite his aristocratic philosophy, Saint-Exupéry found himself beside the Spanish Republicans: he defended this dignity and the unconquerable pride in being a man.

Living in exile in the United States, he might well have added his voice to all those that were raised against the impotent régime of his country, but he chose to express his solidarity with the defeated French and refrained from aggravating their sense of shame. France, for him, was not the collection of corrupt and irresponsible politicians who had led the country to disaster, who having accepted war, were incapable of fighting it, but an old country, with its roots far in the past. It was a nation which over the centuries had grown into a living, corporeal substance that would, one day, reassert itself, if only it stopped believing in 'refrigerators, politics, balance-sheets and crosswords', stopped listening to the robots of propaganda and lent its ear to 'the old village songs of the fifteenth century'.

Saint-Exupéry believes in 'human nature' and eternal values. His nostalgia for a lost France is accompanied by a nostalgia for the old, closed and static communities of the past. In *Citadelle* he imagines a desert kingdom, governed by an absolute monarch who is at once a religious leader, a philosopher and a legislator, ruling over a nation of warriors and artisans. It is a dream quite outside the technological reality of our time and even outside history. Civilization must be judged in relation to man himself.

Man is a 'tension', a 'direction towards', a 'field of forces', a 'desire'. As an individual, he exists no more than a stone in a heap of stones; he exists only in terms of the country he lives in, of a particular enemy; he is a link in a military hierarchy which culminates in the person of the king, who is himself an element in a pyramid whose point is God Himself. He is also a part of the chain of generations past and to come. Living among numerous restrictions, joyously accepted, he experiences his freedom in transcendence. His brothers are not his equals: they live with him in a relationship of command and obedience. His life is original injustice. He binds it to other lives in the name of a common cause which is above them all. He is an element in the home, the trade, the locality, the province, the Empire and they exist outside and contain him as a cathedral contains the stones which constitute it and to which it gives meaning. Life is struggle, transcendence, prayer, a perpetual becoming. It is expressed in the fervent creation of each of us; it is a perpetual exchange. The king himself exists only in relation to God, who gives meaning to the universe.

A civilization disintegrates when the 'divine knot' is untied, when men and things deny their true nature, 'this is what happens when materials mingle together, when glaciers melt into floods, when temples crumble before time, when the heat of the sun becomes lukewarm, when age and usage blur the pages of a book, when language becomes confused and prostituted, when powers are made equal, when effort is standardized and when the divine knot is broken and chaos reigns . . .' Life, says Saint-Exupéry once more, is 'structure, lines of force and injustice'.

The exposition of this philosophy, which lacks neither attraction nor grandeur, has probably done more for Saint-Exupéry's fame than any of his previous works. The French discover in it a reflection of their taste for order and hierarchy – a taste which is constantly vitiated by their temperament, yet constantly renascent. They find in *Citadelle* a desire for change which is contradicted by the means of obtaining it, a yearning for the profound transformation of a society which is moving towards a quite different future, a nostalgia for a legendary past in which everyone would at last find his place in a static, timeless community.

This long incantation reveals a poet and a metaphysician quite foreign to the novels of his time, novels as sober as reportages, as tough as lessons in heroism, dispensers of an energy which triumphed over the worst adversity by an unfailing alliance of patience and courage. It is tempting to think that within Saint-Exupéry there was also a man who was quite ready to turn his back on the all too vulgar problems of his century.

3 *The Theme of War*

If, during the occupation, most novelists remained silent and allowed the poets to take their place, they wasted no time after the liberation in making themselves heard. They were, like the whole of French society, profoundly affected by the war and impatient to make their views known. Among the new works on the war, the concentration camps and the Resistance, there is little that rises to the level of literature. They are often very moving, but their value is no more than documentary. A work of literature requires a certain detachment, a 'disengagement' from the event, a talent which strives, not to restore the confused, accidental, superficial characteristics of reality, but to recreate it in the depths of its nature. The reality of the war was too vast, often too crushing, too stupefying for men who had experienced it to be conscious of it in its entirety. Their personal experience of the war was not enough to provide material for a work of literature. It was necessary first of all to recover one's wits.

The phenomenal aberration of the war, which the French discovered to their horror only when it was all over, was the existence of the Nazi camps – deportation camps, concentration camps, extermination camps – where an immense programme of 'dehumanization' was systematically carried out. It was difficult at first to believe those who had come back: they were accused of exaggerating, even of lying. Later, the truth had to be admitted. It was all so incredible and so obviously a manifestation of evil itself, that few writers felt capable of transforming it into a work that would measure up to their experience. Ten years later, a few writers tried once again, but they too failed to produce more than personal documents. However, the period did produce three writers of genuine talent who have established themselves with impressive and lasting work: David Rousset, Robert Antelme and Jean Cayrol.

David Rousset

On his return from the camps, to which he had been deported as a militant of the extreme left, David Rousset published almost immediately, in 1946, *L'Univers Concentrationnaire*. The work is hardly a novel at all, but it uses fictional devices in a masterly fashion. The title expresses quite clearly the author's intention: to describe a world that is completely cut off from the ordinary world. It is a world that has its own laws, its own finality and is populated by a hitherto unknown species, the *concentrationnaires*. In an attempt to bear witness and at the same time to break through the limitations of documentary evidence, Rousset ignores the traditional techniques of exposition. He plunges us at once into a fantastic, sordid reality which reminds us of Jarry and Kafka. Men and things take on new dimensions. This way of apprehending the least contestable reality involved a form of creation, which, owing to the author's *prise de conscience* and his contrapuntal arrangement of scenes, portraits and anecdotes, goes beyond it. The author is in such complete control of his material that he can carry it outside the actual event and pursue its moral, sociological and metaphysical implications. The camp is a development, logical to the point of caricature, of a certain form of society. It constitutes a monstrous growth, a cancer.

In *Les Jours de Notre Mort,* a much longer work, Rousset is concerned more than ever before to integrate his personal experience into a collective, historical experience. The vast scope of this work reminds one of the Malraux of *L'Espoir* and the Lawrence of *Seven Pillars of Wisdom*.

These works reveal a groping towards the novel-form in so far as they represent a harmonious union of the private and public worlds, in which the two realities confront, balance and interpenetrate one another. David Rousset does not limit himself to describing the world of the concentration camp and formulating its laws. He descends into the depths of consciousness where action and conduct are born. Alternatively, he infers their subjective content from behaviour. He shows men, members of the S.S. or prisoners, who, if they have little in common with humanity, exist in quite different ways from shadows or puppets.

Rousset reveals his attraction for the novel in his choice of technique. He speaks not only of what he has seen and witnessed: he reconstructs the entire phenomenon from the particular aspects of it he has experienced. At once encyclopaedic and didactic, a scientist in his perfect knowledge of his material and an artist in his choice of the elements that compose his work, a novelist in his ability to breathe life into his characters, he could not do better than to use the techniques developed by Dos Passos in *42nd Parallel* and *Manhattan Transfer*. His work is a symphony with themes, leitmotive, recapitulations, pauses, distinct passages of value both in themselves and as parts of the whole, while the movement of the whole is expressed by a feeling of the endless passage of time. We are plunged into an unknown reality in which everything seems foreign to us: the first thing we meet is a scene of mass hanging. This is followed at once by what, in time, preceded it: the deportation of the prisoners from France to Germany. In this way the traditional techniques of autobiography and narrative are destroyed. What takes their place is a reconstruction of a syncopated and ritualized reality. The opening scene has other merits. By describing the voluntary, individual gestures of twelve prisoners in placing the ropes around their own necks, it demonstrates in the best possible way the failure of the system. The entire work illustrates this lesson.

Rousset analyses this system in detail and tries to discover a meaning in it. He shows that although it is based on slavery, starvation and murder, its real basis lies in a 'corruption' that leaves little room for the exercise of traditional morality. For the prisoners, to whom the Nazis offer the poisoned gift of self-administration and who must themselves select those who are to be sent to their deaths, the problem is not to compromise or to refuse; refusal means death. They accept the system, while at the same time trying to preserve the values that give meaning to their lives. For them, it is not a question of self-sacrifice but of self-preservation, so that the ideal of social liberation that they embody can be preserved and remain, even in a state of utter abjection, a guarantee for the future.

The best must be saved. But who will say who the 'best' are? The decision must be that of the underground community as a whole, whose authority these political prisoners accept, voluntarily in this case. The 'leaders' of the community must select from among their comrades those who are to be executed. Some refuse and prefer to kill themselves; for them, 'the victim is as ignoble as the executioner. The one lesson to be learnt from the camps is the brotherhood of shared misery. The difference in the destruction of human beings is one of rhythm.' Yet because of this selection, based on laws of a terrifying logic, the 'strong' survive to witness the collapse of the system. Though degraded to the level of a beast, man refuses to be assimilated in the crude way intended for him. Animated by faith in God or a belief in human progress, he survives and triumphs. Rousset shows that despair is impossible to a man who looks beyond his own life.

Robert Antelme

This fundamental refusal to be entirely dehumanized, this obstinate and silent declaration of humanity, has never been better expressed than in Robert Antelme's *L'Espèce Humaine*, 1947. In contrast to Rousset, Antelme avoids a historical or sociological explanation and refrains from exploiting scenes of horror for aesthetic ends. The result is an essential explanation which attempts to take account of the phenomenon as a human enterprise, in which men, executioners and victims alike, are in some way like ourselves. The work of Robert Antelme is founded upon a questioning that only literature can fully exploit.

Just as he refrains from historical or sociological reconstructions, so he avoids recounting his own experiences. He shows a deportee, himself, submitted to hunger, cold, beatings, moral and physical exhaustion, a pitiful object whose fate is decided by wills other than his own, events quite outside his own control, chance meetings. A second character, who resembles the first like a brother, consciously reflects upon events.

This involves not so much the use of a double-character, as of a technique of alienation, in Brecht's sense of the term. We are transported beyond an account or a description which, however horrible it may be, affects us only obliquely. Horror lived through *as* horror is transformed in the region of experience. Our consciousness identifies itself with the consciousness we see functioning; in the last resort, it is ourselves we are made to pity. The camp is seen to be a place in which humanity, as a biological species and as a product of historical development, is made to face itself in all its fundamental aspects.

The S.S. is dedicated to denying all dependence upon man either as a species or as a historical phenomenon. But its fury is not entirely nihilistic. By its use of eugenics, sterilization, genocide and biological racialism, they are trying to replace nature by their own will, just as by proclaiming a Reich of a thousand years they nurture the insane conviction that they can arrest history. But to establish both claims they need concrete, material proof. The physical extermination of their enemies will not of itself provide them with this proof (though they do have recourse to this). What they need is a perpetual recognition, by their victims, that the notions of humanity and history are meaningless. They desperately need their victims' consent and to obtain this they forge a new type of man, half prisoner and half S.S. – the *kapo*, who is a prisoner by his nature, but who functions as an S.S.

Just when the S.S. think they have won, they have in fact lost: 'the denial of human nature provokes an almost biological claim to belonging to the human race'. This claim is neither moral nor metaphysical, but it possesses the simplicity and the urgency of an absolute. Survival means continuing to live inside one's body; it means, above all, living in full consciousness, while retaining one's solidarity with humanity and history.

Jean Cayrol

Jean Cayrol did not write an account of his life in a concentration camp. He constructed a poetic work of fiction (which he had begun before the war) out of the new vision that a *concentrationnaire* had made of the world, a vision in which feelings, thoughts and concepts had all been overturned. When he returned to normal life he found that man was no longer as he had been before: he would remain a *concentrationnaire* for ever.

For Cayrol the camps were not a historical accident. They were an image of the condition of man on earth expressed in its most extreme form: a condition of utter misery that had to be experienced as a Passion preceding a future Redemption. For the Christian, the *Appelplatz* of the camp was the Garden at Gethsemane: thousands of Christs suffer agony before rising on the resplendent Cross. It is a place of suffering and communion. Those who escape the sacrifice are so many Lazaruses destined to a life of ultimate resurrection. For Cayrol, post-war literature was a Lazarean literature. It bore witness to man's loneliness, his absence in the world, to dereliction, to non-life.

The novel trilogy, the first two volumes of which were awarded the Prix Renaudot in 1947 under the title of *Je vivrai l'Amour des Autres*, was an example of this literature from beyond the tomb. The mouthpiece of the author, Armand, is a drifter, a vagabond in his life and in his feelings. He exists as a shadow and has no more reality than a shadow, clinging to others; too weak even to recognize his own feelings, he lives by procuring 'the love of others'. 'Parasitical love, a Lazarean phenomenon', says Cayrol, 'is not the fear of love, as some might think, but the nostalgia of love in a love without object, in which the carnal is no longer associated with the supernatural, and in this dissociation anything can happen, except creation: it is no more than a product of deception.' Armand experiences the temptation of a double life, 'of another existence over and above that of everyday and which sometimes floods in upon it to such an extent that it appears as a suspicious, unscrupulous fraud'.

He dies in life like a 'stranger'; nothing matters to him, and he is not even capable of entering history; he is quite the opposite of a novel hero. 'Most of us,' says Cayrol, 'are subjects of the Lazarean universe in all its forms. We are consumed by a flame that we did not ourselves light.' Well before the theoreticians of the 'new novel', Jean Cayrol was first to draw attention to the importance of objects in a world in which man is absent. 'The more the Lazarean character is blinded, the more this world of objects sees for him and retains the reflection, the lost sense of the world of one's neighbour. One object placed beside another will be more revealing, more accessible than the human being himself.' Jean Cayrol never forgets that he is a Christian.

The same themes under different forms are to be found again in the works that followed: *La Noire*, 1949, in which a woman constructs a dream of love that leaves her more alone than she had ever been before; *Le Vert de la Mémoire*, 1952; *L'Espace d'une Nuit*, 1954, in which the hero relives his childhood only to realize that it was a failure; *Le Déménagement*, 1956, in which a couple struggle to defend themselves in the strange, fleeting world of objects; *La Gaffe*, 1957, which is the confession of a 'suspicious and unscrupulous' character who relives the pain he experienced when he was deserted by a mistress whom he had not had the strength to love; *Les Corps Etrangers*, 1959, in which a black marketeer of the occupation recalls an incoherent past in which everything he desired had slipped from his grasp; *Le Froid du Soleil*, 1963.

Cayrol's characters give the impression of being unable to anchor themselves to the real world; they float above it, in a dream of their own making. But the strength of the novelist's conviction forces us to wonder if the murky apparitions through which he leads us do not form an important part of our reality; they postulate the arrival of a solid, real world.

The meeting between Jean Cayrol and the phenomenon of the concentration camp would appear to be more than the chance episode of a lifetime: it inspired and fructified a talent that discovered itself because of it and through it.

The war itself (the battles of the end of 1939 and 1940, the general retreat and the embarkation) did not inspire any works comparable with those of Henri Barbusse, Maurice Benevoix or Roland Dorgelès for the previous war. It all happened too quickly and only a small part of the French army was engaged in it. The suffering it caused was soon overcast by much worse suffering, brought about by foreign occupation and captivity. The new phenomenon of the Resistance gave rise to a lot of writing, but for most of the post-war novelists it figures as little more than a series of episodes experienced by characters who seem not to have been much affected by them. Life returned to normal.

Week-end à Zuydcote, by Robert Merle, which was awarded the Prix Goncourt in 1949, is nevertheless more than a simple account of the battle and evacuation of Dunkirk. The author tries to integrate the fate of highly typical characters into the general course of the war, to give his portrayal a range which is really beyond it. In *La Mort est mon Métier*, 1953, he attempts to reconstruct the psychological workings of an executioner in a concentration camp. With *L'Ile*, 1962, perhaps his best book, he deepens his study of the war, in the guise of a maritime adventure in the eighteenth century.

Jules Roy, an ex-bomber pilot, made a noteworthy literary début with *La Vallée Heureuse*, 1946, which relates the daily life and mental conflicts of the bomber pilots whose job was to bombard the cities of the Ruhr each night. A disciple of Saint-Exupéry and Malraux and a friend of Albert Camus, he exemplifies the humanist warrior who finds a certain bitter satisfaction in the fraternity of arms. He can find no glory in a task which he simply considers necessary. Modern war is no longer subject to man's control: the individual man is no more than a robot controlled by death and even his own death, subject to the laws of statistics, is deprived of significance. Jules Roy, an officer and professional airman, is preoccupied by the same questions as are discussed in *Le Métier des Armes*, itself a tardy reply to *Servitude et Grandeur Militaires*. He wants the soldier to be a knight, a cavalier, not a mercenary; he attempted, unreasonably, to introduce this element of chivalry into the least glorious wars, such as the war in Indo-China. He soon exhausted his talent as a novelist and turned to the theatre and to journalism. His anti-colonialist tract, *La Guerre d'Algérie* was a courageous revision of his views.

Jacques Perret is more a storyteller than a novelist. His *Caporal Epinglé* is not so much a novel about being a prisoner of war in Germany as a collection of stories and personal memories. The author has spirit and humour and he knows how to tell a story, as has been proved by the numerous works he has published since and which, with the exception of *Bande à part*, 1951, are all collections of short stories. He is therefore very largely outside the field under discussion.

Romain Gary was inspired not so much by the war as it took place in France as by its effect on Europe. What he wished to express, despite a sometimes clumsy technique, was the malaise of a civilization in decline which could no longer bear the existence of any kind of non-conformist. *Education Européenne*, his first novel, published in 1945, is also his best, despite the award of the Prix Goncourt to a later, well-intentioned but much inferior work, *Les Racines du Ciel*, 1956. In *Education Européenne*, which describes an incident in the Polish resistance, the humanism professed by the author was more justified than in an appeal for the protection of elephants. However, *Tulipe, Le Grand Vestiaire* and *Les Couleurs du Jour*, written between these two works, do communicate a certain sincerity of feeling. *Les Promesses d'Aube*, 1960, is thinly disguised autobiography and *Lady L.*, 1963, an amusing work of satire.

Among the novelists of the Resistance note should be taken of Dominique Ponchardier who, with his *Pavés de l'Enfer*, succeeded in recreating the atmosphere of clandestinity, the dangerous and cruel climate in which its participants lived. The author showed no concern with ideology and the somewhat morbid interest he showed for the 'killers' was soon to take him in the direction of the thriller, in which, under the name of A. L. Dominique, he became highly successful. The only writer truly inspired by the Resistance to establish himself among the best post-war French novelists is Roger Vailland.

Roger Vailland

In 1945 *Drôle de Jeu*, more truly a long short story than a novel, appeared and was noticed at once. It was directly inspired by the Resistance, but stood out among other such works by a tone of calm detachment that reminds one of the seventeenth-century memoir-writers, such as Retz or Saint-Simon, and which made him a curious case of the 'uncommitted' within the 'commitment' of the time. The hero of the story, Marat (his assumed name), believes in the Resistance and takes his struggle against the Germans very seriously. Yet for him the Resistance is only a way of life, imposed upon him by circumstances, a stimulant rather like alcohol or drugs, which takes him out of himself and allows him to live more intensely. Marat is quite willing to sacrifice his life, and he knows that such a sacrifice would not be in vain, but he prefers to remain alive and, taking advantage of the exceptional opportunities offered, makes full use of his potentialities. For life is adventure, unforeseen encounters, danger, love and freedom from moral prohibitions. It is as important for Marat to succeed in a sabotage operation as in the conquest of a pretty woman. This kind of outlaw existence, cut off from normal social life, gives every act and feeling a special savour of its own. Marat sees the Resistance as a 'game' which the man who is free of all ties, the man of superior spirit, can throw himself into.

One must not expect from *Drôle de Jeu* a true picture of the Resistance. The events in which the author took part are no more than a pretext by which he can express his own temperament and philosophy of life – an attitude that contrasts sharply with those of the novelists of the immediate post-war period and one which attempts to revive, a century later, the manner of the eighteenth-century 'libertines' or the 'sensibility', thinly concealed beneath a surface unconcern, of a Stendhal. Roger Vailland admits to being an 'egotist'. Nothing interests him more than his own ego, which he is fond of comparing to those of the individuals he admires.

Consequently, he tries to remain faithful to this dominant trait of his personality, even when it means posing, rather presumptuously, as a 'man of quality', as in his studies of Laclos or the Cardinal de Bernis. However, the reasons that led him to take part in the Resistance drew him in the direction of the Communist Party. Without ever subscribing to the theories of 'socialist realism', he tried to write novels that would serve the working class. In *Bon Pied bon Œil* he praises militance. In *Les Mauvais Coups* he tells the story of the conversion of a libertine to the beauties of trade unionism. In *Beau Masque* he contrasts the futility of bourgeois circles with the seriousness and sense of responsibility of the working class. *325,000 Francs* concerns the impossibility of a worker leaving his own class.

These 'edifying', but very talented works, are drawn in black and white and express a conflict between the two men who co-exist in Vailland himself: the libertine and the communist. The first is sceptical of everything that is not connected with the cult of the ego. The second believes only in social values and in the need for social revolution. Anything that gets in the way of the revolution, like selfishness in love or the pursuit of personal pleasure, must be repressed. And it is always the communist who wins over the libertine. He wins without convincing the reader, who is more interested in the depiction of the vices of the bourgeoisie than in the virtues of communist militants. Conversion has generally something melodramatic about it and strikes rather in the same way as Christian grace. Instead of exalting the convert and enabling him to adopt his new life with joy, it leads him to a 'happy end' and leaves him alone among millions of men whom he wishes to be his brothers, but who are far removed from his own preoccupations.

Just as *Drôle de Jeu* presented a highly personal picture of the Resistance, so the Italy of *La Loi* is a very conventional one: it serves as a picturesque framework, both in its setting and in its values, for what the novelist wishes to express about himself and which in fact seems to express approval of a certain feudalistic state of mind. The hero and spokesman of the writer, Don Cesare, a local potentate whose power seems to extend to the virtue of the village girls, keeps the limelight very much on himself. What is he, if not a libertine as Roger Vailland imagines him to be, as Roger Vailland would himself like to be? It is doubtful whether he would find a place in a communist society. He hasn't even got a place in the world today and is little more than a relic from a previous age. He is 'disinterested' and spends his time in hunting, love and archaeological pot-holing. He is content, as Marx would say, to live off the rents from his property.

Real power, which is economic and financial, has passed into other hands: property owners, politicians, priests, civil servants, even gangsters. And workers are not true workers: they are 'unemployed', leaning all day against the walls of the Place de Porto-Manacore, waiting for work that will probably not materialize.

In this antiquated, timeless society, there is no question of the class struggle. The author replaces it, symbolically, by the game of 'the law' which allows the winners to impose all kinds of penalties on the losers. The author exchanges his old Marxism for an allegory that allows him to reach the only truth that matters to him: the truth of behaviour, and to depict exceptional individuals whose natural qualities he admires: courage, virility, freedom of action and of mind.

Free from his ideological fetters, Roger Vailland constructs a fictional world suitable to an eighteenth-century libertine and atheist who has wandered into a universe disputed by the armed believers in differing faiths. He goes as far as to doubt the necessity, for a novelist, to follow the dictates of 'historical development', or even to concern himself with history at all. In doing so he has undergone a 'conversion' which is the exact opposite of the one he expected.

This is particularly apparent in *La Fête*, 1960, a brilliant story about the seduction of a girl by a *roué*. The man plays his role rather than lives it. He sets himself a task, practises his part and scores points rather like a Laclos hero. His flabbiness, his self-satisfaction, the structural looseness of the novel, with its chunks of *bravura*, lead one to believe that the author has lost the toughness which his communist faith provided him with. In striving unconsciously to fight it, he acquired strength and style. In becoming himself, he has lost these qualities.

4 *The Return of the Pre-War Novelists*

The War, the occupation, the Resistance, the concentration camps had a direct influence on literature and produced a new kind of novel. But these events also provided an opportunity for the previous generation of writers, those who had appeared ten or fifteen years before, to reconsider their work and in some cases it resulted in a considerable revival of their powers. So before introducing the writers who made their names after the war, it would perhaps be useful to consider what had become of those already established. They took up their work, often with increased authority, and played a considerable part in the new post-war literature. Some of them were even canonized.

Louis-Ferdinand Céline

The return to France of Louis-Ferdinand Céline, who had left with the Germans in 1944 and taken refuge in Denmark after the war, had a number of results. The importance of his *Voyage au bout de la Nuit*, published in 1932, was such – he had influenced so many writers (starting with Sartre and Queneau), he had been so obviously at the origin of a certain mode of feeling and writing – that a large proportion of post-war literature would not have existed without him, or at least would have been quite different.

Since *Voyage au bout de la Nuit* and at a time when his contemporaries were still hoping to influence the events that threatened us and calling on man to transcend his condition, Céline was alone in stating a categorical 'no'. No possible salvation existed in a world given up to '*vacherie universelle*' (universal bitchery), no possibility for man to transcend himself. 'The truth of this world is death', and the truth of man is purely and simply a question of saving his own skin. Any means, even the most morally reprehensible, are justified in the struggle to remain in one piece:

lies, treason, cowardice. We did not choose to be what we are: perverted, hypocritical, selfish, lying and, above all, immeasurably cowardly. The world has, is and always will be the scene of organized crime and murder and the poor are always the victims. The only wisdom consists in learning to avoid getting hurt. One succeeds only after practising an infinite number of tricks and apparent acts of submission, then, when the master's back is turned, getting away. Bardamu flees from War, from Africa, from America, from the suburbs, from medicine, from love, from men . . . to Copenhagen. 'One must choose either to die or to lie. I have never succeeded in killing myself.'

This profoundly pessimistic view of society and of man, which was later to have such a great influence, must seem unbearable. It springs from all that is most animal, most visceral in us. The hatred that Céline inspired, and which was fortunate in having political and racial pretexts to hide its real nature, would seem in fact to be organically necessary. Nobody has the right, unless he is himself better than ordinary humanity, to put our noses into our own filth to the point of suffocation. If he assumes this right, then he must suffer the consequences. When Céline spoke of the 'witch-hunt' he was subjected to; when, before his return to France, he complained of being a 'scape-goat', he was not far from the truth.

Yet there is in Céline, especially in *Mort à Crédit*, 1936, a large poetic region where one walks in the gardens of childhood to the sound of sweet music. If the world had not been so 'wicked' if it had given him a chance to live, Céline would have sung moving songs of the past and told fine fairy-tales about the Krogold kings. He dreams of ballets in the moonlight and rustic phantasmagorias. Many of his books, *Le Voyage*, *Mort à Crédit*, *Guignol's Band*, *Féerie pour une autre Fois*, are poems rather than novels: they transform an unbearable reality into a kind of dark, viscous dream. Céline can evoke the early hours of mornings which are to bring all the day's sufferings, the atmosphere of persecuted, misunderstood, martyred childhood, the nostalgia for an impossible escape.

Above all, he shows himself to be a renovator of language. He was the first modern writer to break the rules of literary language, and to write 'as one speaks'. He gave literary dignity to colloquial expression. This spoken language obeys none of the rules of correct speech; it is full of grammatical mistakes, imprecision and repetition, but it is a living, colourful language of flesh and blood which translates emotion and feeling in direct terms. It is very close to exclamation, to the shout and the cry. It brings literary expression back to life. But, of course, Céline is too good a writer to be satisfied with a 'phonographic' language. He submits the spoken language as such to a treatment that breaks it up, sweeps away its fossilized associations and clichés, and when he does not find a phrase ready-made he invents one. He is not a mouthpiece of the man in the street, but Louis-Ferdinand Céline, who follows his own rhythm.

The Céline of the post-war period is no longer the Céline of *Le Voyage* and *Mort à Crédit*. His invention has become laborious, his verbal felicities only too expected and his technique has degenerated into mannerism. For the few amazing pages to be found in *D'un Château l'autre*, 1957, and above all in *Nord*, 1960, there are hundreds of lifeless ones, full of inflated rhetoric (even if it is Céline's), intentional naïveties and depressing futilities. A reading of these last works leads one to wonder if this writer of genius had anything more than average talent. His decline is moving in itself: it is the result of a long process of self-destruction. Unlike many writers, Céline believed in what he wrote.

Georges Bernanos

During the war, Georges Bernanos went into exile in Brazil. He came back as soon as the war was over and took up the pamphleteering vein of *La Grande Peur des Bien-pensants*, 1931, and *Grands Cimetières sous la Lune*, 1938. He published only one more novel, *Monsieur Ouine*, written in 1943, which possesses neither the inspiration nor the style of *Sous le Soleil de Satan,* 1926, or the *Journal d'un Curé de Campagne*, 1936. On the creative plane he turned rather to the theatre, for which he wrote his last work, *Dialogue des Carmélites*, 1948.

Bernanos, a Christian and a novelist, is not a Christian novelist. The expression is too often associated with dull didacticism, whereas Bernanos, with his ingenious manipulation of thriller-type plots, the power of his vision and his preoccupation with salvation and spiritual values is closer to another novelist who, we have come to forget, was also a Christian: Dostoyevsky. Having neither Dostoyevsky's power nor his unpredictable genius, he established himself as one of the most important novelists of his generation. He exercised a particular influence upon two younger writers, Luc Estang and Jean Cayrol.

If, for Bernanos, the Christian universe of grace and charity really did exist, he was even more aware of the world as a scene of struggle, of 'the battle of souls' against the works of the devil (who has dominion over this world), and it is a struggle, if not without hope, at least without end. This struggle justifies man: while ever it lasts, all is not lost. When it ceases, honour and dignity cease with it. Even souls that have fallen entirely under the sway of the devil are capable at some time or another of repentance and of being forgiven by the Father. Grace is visited upon all who merit it, even the most fallen.

At first sight the field covered by Bernanos the novelist might seem less wide than that of Bernanos the polemicist, who deals with every aspect, including social and political ones, of the modern world. His heroes are often priests, and the world in which they move is a clerical world. This is because, for Bernanos, the priest represents a privileged region in which Good and Evil confront each other and his sacramental function in no way protects him from human weakness. Unlike many Catholic novelists, Bernanos is not interested in the priest's failings (sin) for themselves, but for the tension they create in the soul struggling towards God and for the often unexpected ways they present of reaching Him. The worst sin is indifference: indifference towards oneself, indifference towards salvation. This is the sickness of Monsieur Ouine, in the novel that bears his name. Like a cancer that eats away the individual, indifference spreads over the world and turns man into a being devoid of feeling, a robot. If forced to choose, the novelist would prefer to see man possessed by the devil.

Man is not only a 'soul'. He participates in three essential realities: biological, by his ties with family, region and nation; social, by the fact of his belonging to a community based upon faith and tradition; and spiritual, by his need to transcend his condition. If he lacks one of these components or if he tries to deny any of them, he loses his humanity and becomes an 'imbecile' that is to say a simple social, economic, political or religious object. Moreover, he needs to feel 'honourable' and 'free'. Bernanos' theology is founded upon a humanism, or at least postulates one. Bernanos has this in common with many post-war novelists: he tries to depict man in his physical reality, in the expression of his instincts and in the midst of a geographical, social and religious environment, concealing no aspect of the truth. He also shares with them a pessimistic view of a world doomed to disintegration, of man allowing himself to sink more and more into material, intellectual and moral comfort. The role of the novelist, like the parallel role of the pamphleteer, is not so much didactic as denunciatory. Neither has much faith in rationalism, or in what they contemptuously call 'realism'. Both have the power to move: one by the fervour of his language, the other by the intensity of his vision.

Jean Giono

After the war, the author of *Un de Baumugnes, Le Grand Troupeau, Jean Le Bleu*, a prophet of the return to nature and a militant pacifist, was condemned to a temporary silence. He emerged in 1950 transformed. During his enforced retirement he had written some ten works, which he now published one after another. They bore little resemblance to his earlier pastoral rhapsodies of the shepherds and peasants of Haute-Provence. Giono had become a novelist who tried to compose complicated and mysterious stories, to create real characters, to convey the feel of life itself. *Noé*, a kind of poetic journal, still bears the marks of the earlier period, but *Un Roi sans Divertissement, Mort d'un Personnage, Les Ames Fortes*, and above all *Le Hussard sur le Toit*, 1951, *Le Moulin de Pologne*, 1952, *Le Bonheur Fou*, 1957, are real novels, often with complicated plots, in which the characters exist in their own right and retain their own secret life. One of the most endearing, Angelo Pardi, whose adventures during an epidemic of cholera that laid waste the Haute-Provence in 1838 (*Le Hussard sur Le Toit*) or during the ups and downs of a revolution in Italy in 1848 (*Le Bonheur Fou*), aspires to being a spiritual grandson of Stendhal and is closely related to Fabrice del Dongo. He has Fabrice's youth, his generosity of feeling, a love of personal glory and the same lust for happiness. When he sets out on an adventure, it is to test his strength, his courage, his virility and will-power. The characters that succeed him possess the same simple tension: Giono is not concerned with psychological subtleties. Created to the same pattern, they all seem to be charged with a 'mission', into which they throw themselves wholeheartedly, determined to destroy everything that comes in their way. They pursue their courses as if they were on rails, irrespective of whether, from a moral point of view, their objective is right or wrong. Giono's works are peopled by the 'strong', some destined for good, and others destined for evil; what is important is that they should be 'strong'.

Giono is little concerned with verisimilitude and the situations he describes are often scarcely credible. He could even be accused of falling into melodrama. What he is really aiming at is tragedy, classical tragedy with its choruses and recitatives. The old Giono, who tried to raise ordinary events of village life to the grandeur of epic, has not entirely been effaced. But this grandeur is now provided more by history than by folklore and the old poet of the earth and the stars turns more and more to historical reconstruction. This escape into the past saves Giono from having to take sides in the controversies of our time and allows him even more than before to turn away from a world that has disappointed him and which he totally rejects.

Louis Aragon

Aragon emerged from the struggles of the occupation and the Resistance a national hero. During the war, the ex-Surrealist had become the official bard of occupied France. But the official poet was also a novelist with two titles to his name, *Les Cloches de Bâle* and *Les Beaux Quartiers*, both published before the war. In 1945 he published *Aurélien* and in 1947 the definitive edition of a book published in 1943 and which the Germans had banned, *Les Voyageurs de l'Impériale*. Aragon considered these two works to be the natural successors to the novels published before the war. They were attempts at conveying a true image of 'real life'.

Despite his political beliefs, Aragon might be thought of as an excellent bourgeois novelist. He is interested less in the world of labour than in the world from which he himself sprang and which continues to occupy a considerable part of his mind. In *Les Voyageurs de l'Impériale*, a fresco of the Third Republic in which we study the activities of businessmen, politicians and members of the upper classes, the novelist's eye is sufficiently sharp to penetrate appearances, to detect the real motives underlying actions and to denounce deception and hypocrisy. In this sense it is a work of denunciation, but curiously enough there is an absence of any feeling of revolt. *Aurélien*, a kind of filigree based on the author's own childhood, is even more nostalgic in tone and fails to conceal a certain regret for the past.

As the spokesman in France of the theory of 'socialist realism', Aragon was obliged to set a good example. He undertook to recount in a series of novels the struggles, anxieties and victories of his political friends. However, in his *Communistes*, of which only the first few volumes appeared, historical truth is so mishandled, the characters are so vague and improbable, even the writing itself so foreign to the author, that he did not persevere in his self-imposed task. He chose to return to his first loves and, in 1958, to almost universal critical acclaim, he published *La Semaine Sainte*.

Despite the author's denials, *La Semaine Sainte* is a historical novel which relates the flight of Louis XVIII and the Royalists prior to Napoleon's return. The author did research on the period over a number of years and knows every detail of his subject down to the colours of the uniforms of each regiment of the Royalist army. He excels in the building up of set pieces and he is a master at providing historical characters with credible psychological conflicts. His hero, the painter Géricault, who might well have been lost among such a multitude of characters, succeeds in capturing the reader's interest. What one admires in this novel is not so much the talent of the novelist as that of the fresco painter and the qualities of the composition. Another dimension is given to the work by the faint echoes of contemporary events: the exodus of 1940, the flight of the retreating Germans and the confessions with which the author interlards his narrative. Yet the narration itself is subject to so many conventions culled from different sources, from Alexandre Dumas or from the nineteenth-century pamphleteers, that it seems to have been written quite outside the context of our times. Not the least paradoxical thing about this brilliantly talented and technically perfect work is that it was written by a communist.

Louis Guilloux

Louis Guilloux began his literary career, about 1930, with a number of part documentary, part fictional novellas. Guilloux was born into a poor family and was soon attracted by left-wing ideas. His first works, *Maison du Peuple*, 1927, *Compagnons*, 1930, *Hyménée*, 1931, depict the lives of workers and trade unionists. *Le Sang Noir*, a work of more ambitious proportions, has as its setting the political struggles of a provincial town and as hero an eccentric, rather lovable schoolmaster. During the war he published *Pain des Rêves*, which recounts the author's own childhood, and, in 1949, *Le Jeu de Patience*, in which, in the form of apparently random notes, he sketches a picture of provincial life and its relations with the great events of the inter-war years. *Les Batailles Perdues*, 1960, is a new *Jeu de Patience* which reveals Guilloux above all as an accomplished storyteller.

The works of Louis Guilloux are closer to reportage than to fiction. Their author is guided by a concern for truth and he wishes above all to recreate the feel and colour of life as it is lived from moment to moment. The narrator is always a witness: he refuses to bend the story to serve his own ends and refrains from intervening in the fate of his characters and in the choice of their acts. As a result, his works give an impression of naturalness, not to say carelessness, an absence of composition and architecture which seem to spring from the free course of life itself. The author wishes to be no more than a compère, who presents his characters, allows them to speak, then whisks them off. In any case, he differs from the historian and journalist in so far as his characters are seen from the inside. Their actions, or the accounts he gives of them, do have a meaning: Guilloux exposes the poverty, the suffering, the struggles and the loneliness of those who find themselves at the bottom of the social ladder. He exalts the solidarity of the working masses and the brotherhood and devotion of their leaders. He resists, fortunately, the temptation to preach: he always leaves the reader to make up his own mind. His latest works make incursions into a literature that is less subject to its content (*Parpagnacco*, 1954), even if, here and there, a few notes of muted despair are to be heard.

André Dhôtel

André Dhôtel, who came upon the literary scene in 1930 with his *Campements*, is a writer, who, in spite of having some twenty novels to his name, remained for a long time relatively unknown. The award of the Prix Fémina as late as 1955 for *Le Pays où l'on n'arrive jamais*, brought him at last to the forefront.

There are few novelists whose works give such an impression of similarity. The action often centres on one of those mystery plays that used to be presented in the evenings in certain villages. The extraordinary characters are at one with an atmosphere that is imbued with a feeling for natural poetry and dream.

At first sight Dhôtel does not seem to break the laws of strict realism. He 'names' places, things, individuals and events – even with what might be considered an excessive taste for detail. He limits himself to describing the behaviour of his characters, but they are nearly all in some way or another eccentric. He tells stories, but they are all confused and confusing. So much so that his 'realism' is constantly falling over into 'irrealism', not to say 'surrealism', without our really being aware of it. In the most natural way imaginable he turns the ordinary into the marvellous. What Dhôtel is probably doing is restoring the atmosphere of childhood, with its freedom, its contempt of consequences and its absence of responsibility.

In all Dhôtel's novels there is a child or adolescent, who, by some unconscious act of revolt, breaks down the power of conformity, upsets the fixed habits of his environment and in some subtle way alters the atmosphere around him. Just as the author twists appearances to the point of piercing the mirror, so the characters of *Un Village Pathétique, Rues dans l'Aurore, L'Homme de la Scierie* and *Plateau de Mazagran* discover beyond appearances, in life itself, an end and a justification for their existence. The village can-can is transformed into a *chanson de geste* or an epic. The novel can still be a story of marvellous adventures, with characters carried off, disappearances, unexpected meetings and amazing happenings. As conceived by Dhôtel, it resembles a story told by a child who gradually allows his imagination full rein. The artist is behind the child, guiding him according to the rules of a subtle and enchanting artistry.

5 *Surrealism and after*

As a living movement surrealism belongs to the inter-war period. It never became a literary school, but it deeply affected the climate of ideas, feelings and artistic expression, and, in fifteen years, gave new life to each of the arts and broke down the barriers that separated them from each other. Surrealism was particularly fruitful in poetry and painting. It produced few novelists.

It is even less surprising that André Breton, the leader and chief theoretician of the movement, always considered the novel as a minor form and as the refuge of *littérateurs*. For surrealism was largely a reaction against 'literature', and for a deeper and more direct expression of the strange, the marvellous and the unconscious in all its manifestations. Breton believed that the novel had never succeeded in getting out of its naturalistic and psychological rut and it was Breton who was responsible for Paul Valéry's famous phrase: '*Je me refuserai toujours à écrire: la marquise sortit à cinq heures*'.

Yet at a time when the novel was most open to attack and even as a result of these attacks, it was evolving and altering its form. Instead of being simply a 'story' or, worse, 'a slice of life', it became proteiform, a *genre* capable almost of absorbing all others – lyrical prose, poem, confession, manifesto. The traditional rules that had been more or less codified at the end of the nineteenth century were completely abandoned. Any fiction was now a novel. The label was used merely to differentiate any work that was obviously a product of the writer's imagination from reportage, documentary writing, journalism. But, of course, the distinction between what was and was not a novel remained vague – some novelists even prided themselves on the fact that they used the fictional form only to express reality itself, to recreate more fully a sense of life as it is really lived, and refused to invent anything. The definition of the novel was so changeable that Gide denied writing novels at all, and accepted as such only *Les Faux Monnayeurs*, even though this book was no less or no more a novel than, say, *Les Caves du Vatican*. Malraux acknowledged himself to be a novelist, but he certainly thought of *L'Espoir* as being more than a novel. And how are we to label the works of Leiris and Beckett?

With the frontiers of the form being pushed ever farther outwards, and the novel becoming more and more a field for freedom of expression, it would have been surprising indeed if the influence of surrealism had not made itself felt. If, in the real sense of the term, there are no surrealist novelists – the excessively controlled form of a Julien Gracq or the precious, highly-wrought prose of a Mandiargues contradicts the canons of automatic writing – there are, none the less, novelists (in the wide sense of the term) who, having been members or fellow-travellers of the surrealist group, have made use of its discoveries and carried the spirit of the movement into their works. They have retained the same taste for the strange and the marvellous, the same desire for freedom, the same tendency to abandon worn-out modes, whether in life or in literary expression, the same desire to change, at one and the same time, 'life' and 'the world', in short, to discover and use writing as an instrument in the profound transformation of Being. Not every surrealist characteristic is to be found in each of them. But each has taken from surrealism what was most suited to his own needs.

Georges Limbour

Expelled from the surrealist group for his lenient attitude towards 'literature', Georges Limbour is perhaps rather more a poet or storyteller than a novelist. As a young man, he was a friend of Max Jacob, who did much to make his name known. However, he had to wait another twenty-five years before his first volume of verse, *Soleil Bas*, was rediscovered by Aragon and

Cocteau, who publicly acknowledged him as one of their masters.

In 1930 he published under the title of *L'Illustre Cheval Blanc* a collection of short stories that had been written many years before. These were followed by novels that were charged with poetry, irony and feeling: *Les Vanilliers*, 1938, *La Pie Voleuse*, 1939, and *Le Bridge de Madame Lyane*, 1948. Since then Limbour began once more to write stories and became interested in art criticism. He had come to accept the fact that his work remained relatively unknown, when in 1963 *La Chasse au Mérou* suddenly brought him to the forefront of attention.

Georges Limbour is of an essentially poetic temperament and his natural talent is best expressed in creating an atmosphere of magic and the marvellous which envelopes objects, events and characters. Yet the illusion he creates, with such apparently simple means, is securely tied to ordinary, everyday life, to a reality in which the great events and the great fears of the period are felt. *Les Vanilliers*, which is imbued with the exotic atmosphere of a colony in the eighteenth century, does nothing to hide the hard lives of the workers on the vanilla estates. *La Pie Voleuse*, which describes life in a Spanish village before and after the Civil War, is a denunciation of the war itself. *Le Bridge* takes place in the Balkans at the time when these countries were about to be turned upside down by the Second World War. Over the Spain of *La Chasse au Mérou* reigns a sordid 'callipygian tyrant'.

The strange and the marvellous are not for this writer a means of escape. They spring naturally and directly from a reality that contains them: usually unperceived, they are none the less a part of this reality. Despite its discreet, graceful and ironic tone, Georges Limbour's voice possesses a fairly extended register. Among the choir of post-war voices, his continues to sing its own song.

Raymond Queneau

Raymond Queneau was a surrealist for many years. In 1929, when the group underwent its most serious crisis, he remained among the faithful who supported the expulsions announced by André Breton in the *Deuxième Manifeste du Surréalisme*. Some months later, however, he broke with Breton. After studying the subject of the clown in literature (the results of which he incorporated in *Enfants du Limon*, published in 1938), he published, in 1933, his first novel, *Le Chiendent*. Others followed, alternating with volumes of verse. *Les Derniers Jours*, 1936, *Odile*, 1937, *Un Rude Hiver*, 1939, *Pierrot, Mon Ami*, 1946, *Loin de Rueil*, 1944, *Le Dimanche de la Vie,* 1951 and, finally, *Zazie dans le Métro*, 1959, which, unexpectedly, placed him in the best-seller lists. Meanwhile, he was elected to the Académie Goncourt.

The work of Raymond Queneau, the poet, is at least as important as his work as a novelist. Both, however, were ignored by the general public until after the war. His name attained a certain notoriety with *Exercices de Style*, 1947, which seemed at first sight, however, to be no more than a rhetorical game. In fact, its freedom of invention was itself a source of provocation. A Saint-Germain-des-Prés cabaret was made of the work and success came at last.

Raymond Queneau has retained from his surrealist days a taste for the humorous and ridiculous aspects of ordinary life. He takes us into the working-class suburbs, with their fairs and circuses, where the work-begrimed inhabitants take life as it is without concerning themselves with its great problems. But the writer does concern himself with the problems and, without them knowing it, makes his characters live the problem of existence (its why and its how), the problem of passing time, the problems of old age and death and the problems caused by the innumerable cares that beset the simple and anonymous at every moment. *Le Chiendent* was modelled on Descarte's *Discours de la Méthode* and *Le Dimanche de la Vie* begins with an exegesis of Hegel. Behind his simple, childlike façade, Queneau is a highly conscious writer, passionately interested in philosophy and mathematics, who seems to abandon himself to chance inspiration only when he has some higher end in view. The humorist conceals a disillusioned, rather bitter and pessimistic philosopher.

Nor did Queneau approach the novel without preparation. He is a great admirer of Flaubert, the Flaubert of *Bouvard et Pécuchet*, with whom he shares the same amused delight in human stupidity, in received ideas, in the conventions of social life and derives the same bitter pleasure in depicting them. His study of the techniques of novel construction led him to give many of his works a circular form, either closed in upon themselves, as in *Le Chiendent*, or open to the future, as in *Odile* or *Les Derniers Jours*. In his theoretical writings, collected in *Bâtons, Chiffres et Lettres*, 1950, he insisted upon the fact that one could never become a novelist without possessing and practising a technique, that nothing in a novel should be left to chance. The novelist must possess a sense of discipline, a concern for architecture and construction, unremitting devotion to the task of composition. Yet at the same time these various conscious concerns must not be apparent in the work itself, which must appear to be subject to no other than natural necessity, even though this 'nature' is, in fact, an effect of art.

Apart from a deep admiration for the ancestor of all literature, Homer, Queneau has revealed his spiritual fathers: James Joyce, Louis-Ferdinand Céline, Charles Péguy and, to a lesser degree, Marcel Proust. He has learnt something from each of them: from some how to express action in terms of passing time (the novel is essentially about the passing of time), from others, especially Joyce and Céline, the need to forge one's own instrument, a language of one's own. Like Joyce, he wished to create words that are not to be found in any dictionary and yet which alone correspond to what the writer wishes to express. Like Céline, he wished to deliver a mortal blow to conventional language (literary language sometimes degenerating into academic language). He condemns the language-police, trained by schools and universities, by the humanities and by readings of the classics and the great writers of the past. Faced with a new writer, the 'police' announces prohibitions and formulates taboos. Against this convention of literary language, Raymond Queneau exalts the perpetual, overflowing language of speech, which is emotional, visceral, real. He absorbs unusual, earthy or picturesque words from popular speech and slang. He breaks up syntax to bring it closer to spoken language. He tries to spell words as they are pronounced. But he does not carry his revolution to the point of creating obstacles to communication. On the contrary, his aim is to make communication easier, more natural, more real.

Because of this self-conscious side of Raymond Queneau's art, he has, paradoxically, been thought of as a sort of mandarin, an inventor of intellectual games. Beneath the apparent haphazardness, the humour and the oddness of his novels, many people felt the presence of a desire to communicate on another plane, in another dimension. In one way or another, his works eluded the reader. This is no less true of *Zazie dans le Métro*, but it is unlikely that all the hundred thousand readers of this book were aware of the fact. It is simply that the action moves in a more rapid, a more obvious way, carrying one on before one has even had time to get alarmed or ask questions. While experienced readers of Queneau can linger over the subtleties, a much greater number can derive a simple, relaxed pleasure from this work, thanks to the unusual characters, the development of the crazy but pitiless logic of the situations, but above all to the expressions, taken from popular speech, which immediately became famous.

Nevertheless, Raymond Queneau remains for the critic a problem which requires a great deal of analysis. It has been attempted. One may well wonder if his work represents a negation of literature, a contempt for it, or simply an exaggeratedly literary monument. Arguments can be found equally well for all three theses. What is certain, however, is that Queneau's relations with literature and with the novel are not innocent ones. His work lies at the heart of the problems which have arisen in our time regarding the relation between literature and life and between expression and communication. If he has found a solution for himself, he has kept it well hidden: it is not to be found in his own comments on his work. It is probably this that has given his work a paradoxically esoteric appearance.

Michel Leiris

Michel Leiris, an ex-member of the surrealist group and, like Queneau, a poet, would certainly not consider himself to be a novelist. His most important works, in which fiction is mingled with autobiography in a kind of mythical creation that transcends both, are nevertheless of such importance and exercise such a deep influence on the young writers of today that the conventional boundaries of the form must be stretched to admit them. It may even be that Michel Leiris has founded a new literary *genre* beside which the traditional *genres* – novel, journal, confession – are shown to be inadequate and limiting. He has not only given his own answers to the pressing questions that literature has been asking for twenty years: he has shown a way.

Like all the surrealists, Michel Leiris began by writing accounts of dreams and 'automatic' poems. Like them, he was intrigued by certain properties of language, in particular by its power of instantly producing thought. One has only to change the order of the words in some common expression, or to reverse the terms of a proverb for a new, surprising meaning to appear. The simple fact of bringing words together by alliteration or assonance also produces unexpected, sometimes fascinating results. The *jeux de mots*, or puns, used so much by Marcel Duchamp, Paul Eluard and Robert Desnos are taken systematically by Michel Leiris, who extracts from them more than merely amusing results.

In fact he took Breton's saying, that 'literature should lead somewhere', seriously. He expects literature to have certain aims, the most important of which is the total involvement of the writer in his medium. Having revealed the erotic, tragic, perhaps mystical substructure of an ordinary bull-fight, Leiris proceeds to demonstrate that literature is itself a tauromachy, a certain kind of ceremony, with its own rituals and rules, which ends with an execution and involves all the risks of such an ending. The writer may not be a bull-fighter; but if he refuses to involve himself as a bull-fighter does, in a dangerous and ritualistic struggle with what he has to say about himself and about the world, he is making use of literature in a futile and superficial way.

The first result of such an aesthetic is that the writer becomes his own material. He publicly compromises himself by revealing what a writer is never expected to reveal: his own impulses, instincts, fantasies, his personal mythology, even the peculiarities of his physical and physiological organism. *L'Age d'Homme*, which Michel Leiris published in 1939, renewed the form of the confession and caused a transformation in depth of the content of post-war French literature. The work is conceived as a psycho-analytical confession, but its importance lies in the artistic synthesis that the author has made of the materials revealed in analysis. The reader is led by this contagious example to make his own analysis and history of his personal mythology, the stuff out of which he has unconsciously built his life, his behaviour and his view of the world.

After the war, Michel Leiris began a work of monumental proportions, *La Règle du Jeu*, of which only two volumes have appeared, *Biffures* in 1948 and *Fourbis* in 1955. It is symptomatic that having to choose a label for these works, he called them *essais*, wishing it to be understood, presumably, that these were not works of 'fiction'. In fact, Leiris is speaking about himself, in the most precise, circumstantial and sincere way possible. They are essays in the sense of Montaigne's essays, or, nearer to ourselves, of Marcel Jouhandeau's *Essai sur moi-même*.

Having chosen to speak of himself, to find the material of his work within himself, the writer cannot see himself, does not even wish to see himself through the eyes of an objective observer. He participates in the observation and is involved in it, the degree of involvement being for Leiris the very reason for writing. The role of 'fiction' here lies precisely in that, instead of repudiating invention, imagination and mythification, the writer makes use of them in constructing something that should be neither a scientific or medical report, nor a journal of everyday life, but a work of art. One might even go further and say that for Leiris this end is itself a secondary one. Carrying his investigation still further, he believes that the work should be the man himself, the writer, provided with new dimensions, not merely his reflection, but the creation to which he attains, starting from himself, through the medium of writing. At the same time, the gap is filled between what is expressed and he who expresses it, between literature and life, artistic creation and reality. The importance of Michel Leiris' achievement is that it provides an answer that is not merely personal to the questions that literature poses today. It is a valuable example for all writers, at least for those who have not chosen merely to entertain and amuse. It is a proof of the affirmation that literature should 'lead somewhere'.

Biffures, like *Fourbis*, has its point of departure in the phenomena of language, mysterious, aberrant, as perceived by children for the first time. An ordinary word or expression, repeated by a child, crystallizes feelings, ideas and actions which give the word or expression a significance that is often far removed from its true meaning. An emotional atmosphere, or 'aura', forms around the word or expression that, coloured by fear or desire, becomes the bearer of a certain reality. When the writer tries to penetrate to the nature of this reality, he discovers an instinctive, emotional, mythological substructure which is identified with himself, with the vision he has of the world and in which he gravitates. Gradually, with the help of the man he has become, he builds the unique structure which bears his name, expresses his personality and answers for him before others. The material is supplied by the memory and the retrospective illumination of the past. Carefully making his way into the dark labyrinth, he stumbles from time to time upon great expanses of light. Discovering himself, he begins to build. Instead of being a mere product of his activity as a writer, the work co-operates in the development of a self and marks its different stages. The transforming activity of writing has never been better described, nor better proof given of this metamorphosis.

Fourbis shows that the world of the adult is little different from the world of the child. Despite a rational and sometimes reasoning activity, despite the pressure from a world that demands typical behaviour, the adult lives in a phantasmagoria. He is much more at home in this fantasy world than he is in the rational categories in which he is obliged to move. Michel Leiris is not content to analyse this phantasmagoria: he recreates it through the multitude of circumstances in which it is revealed; he sees it whole and gives it a new, secondary existence. To the task that Proust has accomplished so brilliantly, he adds another, incomparably more difficult one, of bringing to life, in a plausible incarnation, the private, collective and ancestral myths that lie behind his actions.

In doing this, he also breaks down the frontiers of the self. Relating the man he has been, or is, to the world which often pulls the strings, he also goes beyond the limits of the confession and of the novel, to arrive at a significant and conscious equivalent of that world. The reader can only suppose this structure to be indestructible. Thus a literary phenomenon has become a phenomenon of the world itself. There is scarcely a literary opus today that can compare in authenticity and stature to that of Michel Leiris.

Julien Gracq

Julien Gracq was drawn to surrealism by André Breton himself, but he belongs to a later generation than Limbour, Queneau and Leiris. He did not participate in the glorious events of the movement's heyday, his first book, *Au Château d'Argol*, being published in 1938. Seven years later, in 1945, he published *Un Beau Ténébreux*, then, in 1951, *Le Rivage des Syrtres* (for which he refused the Prix Goncourt) and, in 1958, *Un Balcon en Forêt*. He is also the author of a book of poems in prose, *Liberté Grande* and a play, *Le Roi Pêcheur*.

Julien Gracq is a scrupulous, polished and intentionally solemn writer. He strives after a beautiful prose that is stylized, hieratic and strongly evocative. Every word, every phrase is measured in its effect. Here already was a quality which was likely to please André Breton, who was himself a highly conscious prose-writer. Breton also appreciated in Gracq's work its power to lead one by a kind of hypnosis into a highly romantic atmosphere. The author of *Au Château d'Argol* and *Un Beau Ténébreux* has borrowed from the French Romantics, and even more so from the German Romantics, a whole range of terror and mystery: old castles, mysterious forests, nocturnal apparitions, fatal and thwarted love, a taste for adventures that require a hopeless physical or emotional commitment, a desire for escape beyond earthly bounds, a thirst for the unknown. Beneath the apparent smoothness of language there seethes a world of desires, dreams and more or less infernal incantations. Man is drawn out of his everyday world into a mystic, pagan beyond which he believes to be his real home.

Seeking inspiration in an even more distant past, in the Middle Ages of the Holy Grail, or in the struggling towns of the Italian renaissance (*Le Rivage des Syrtes*), Julien Gracq follows a thread which runs through all his works, the use of simple description or evocation. As for the Knights of the Grail, it is the thread which leads to a justification of man by the acceptance of an unknown destiny. This destiny is revealed to him in certain privileged circumstances and signifies the obscure presence of salvation. Gracq knows how to place the reader in an atmosphere of expectancy and preparation for the discovery of the marvellous. When he chooses not to go beyond the merely unusual, our disappointment is proportional to the excitement and depth of feeling he has aroused in us.

Both the manner and the sources of the inspiration of Julien Gracq place him apart from contemporary novelists, who are generally more concerned to develop in a world that is closer to our problems and anxieties. Nevertheless, he did try to do just this in *Un Balcon en Forêt* which is about a real event in the 'phoney war'. But even here the novel is set in the forest of the Ardennes, which is traditionally rich in mystery, and the woman who appears in the forest could be no other than a new avatar of Melusina. The action could equally well take place anywhere, at any time, and with other characters. Julien Gracq has no desire to cross the frontiers of his own world, so rich in surprises and poetic mysteries.

André Pieyre de Mandiargues

André Pieyre de Mandiargues, who was also recognized by André Breton as being a surrealist writer, is a poet and storyteller rather than a novelist. His first works were published, during the occupation, in Monaco, where he was living as a refugee. A series of short stories, somewhat precious and fantastic, yet possessing a highly-wrought form, were collected and later published under the title *Dans les Années Sordides*. Other collections followed: *Le Musée Noir*, 1946, *Soleil des Loups* (which was awarded the Prix des Critiques in 1951), *Marbre*, 1953. Two later works, *Le Lis de Mer*, 1956 and *La Motocyclette*, 1963, depart even further from the the traditional novel forms.

Pieyre de Mandiargues is haunted by 'mystery' in all its forms: the mystery that envelops the creations of man and of nature and the mystery one meets in ordinary, everyday life. He detests whatever is banal, ordinary, expected, or mass-produced. He is an aesthete, a decadent in the *fin-de-siècle* sense. He enthuses over a single detail in a picture, the ornamental motif of a piece of furniture or the strange shape of a rock. The 'strangeness' of an object is not for him the sign of some mysterious presence and refers to nothing beyond itself. It exists by itself and for itself; the pleasure it arouses is purely aesthetic. Like all manifestations of the baroque spirit in our industrial, utilitarian society, it bears witness to the unlimited possibilities of man when free from the demands of the world he lives in and to his desire to escape from this world. It acts in our society as a safety valve.

To these aberrational manifestations of the 'strange', Mandiargues adds the constructions of his own imagination. He creates his own monsters and chimeras, human beings who have been touched by the angel of the bizarre. He moves in an atmosphere of fantasy, and has recourse neither to sorcery nor terror – means which he would reject as too crude. The aesthetic response is always uppermost, and the emotional thrill it causes is one of surprise. When the inspiration of the writing is erotic, or involves a certain brutality, Mandiargues succeeds in enveloping it in an atmosphere of urbanity.

Nevertheless, he is not a delicate or reassuring writer. Sometimes, in the interstices of a polished sentence, chiselled like a valuable knick-knack, passes a sulphurous whiff from some inferno. The influence of German romanticism – that of Achim von Arnim, rather than that of Novalis – is apparent in this writer's work. Mandiargues has latinized it, sometimes even Italianized it, cleansing it of its more obvious puerilities, while retaining its strength.

6 *Metamorphoses of the Novel*

Even prior to 1940 a change was apparent in the *Zeitgeist* that affected literature as much as other modes of thought. The literature created by such masters as Gide, Claudel, Valéry, Montherlant, Giraudoux and, for the younger generation, by Malraux, Giono and Bernanos was showing signs of fatigue.

The revival of the novel in the thirties had produced a number of outstanding works. But certain agonizing questions had still not been resolved. Novelists had seen salvation as coming from social revolution, religion or a return to nature: their solutions, coming at the time when Hitler's big drums were beginning to beat, were cruelly out of date. They would have to confront the gathering storm, naked and unarmed. What values could they go on defending? Some, like the humanism of Gide and Valéry, or the panic Catholicism of Claudel, seemed spent. Others were denounced and trampled under foot by the gangs of a hysterical dictator. Literature, thought and philosophy seemed to be struck dumb. In the glow of Nazi incendiarism, two contradictory, but related phenomena appeared: a scepticism, which soon turned into complete indifference and despair, and a furious appetite for the elementary life, for the instinctive, for animal brutality.

The transformation did not take place at once. The intelligentsia tried to forget the problems it should have resolved and sought temporary refuge in futility or mysticism. It was a time when a play by Giraudoux, produced by Louis Jouvet at the Théâtre de l'Athénée, provided a pleasurable interlude between two of Hitler's ultimatums, and when Messrs. Romains and Maurois were regarded as thinkers. Elsewhere, there were a number of notable conversions to the esoteric teachings of India, to Tibetan mysticism, or, more usually, to Catholicism. Attention was directed abroad and help from any source was welcomed.

In the field of fiction, one no longer expected help from Russia, who was now engaged in building up a literature that reflected her own rather special preoccupations. The last of her great poets, Mayakovsky, had committed suicide. A few important novelists, such as Boris Pilniak and Isaac Babel, had disappeared, either shot or deported. Although Dostoyevsky and the Tolstoy of *War and Peace* still received attention, the technical problems that concerned them no longer seemed to be relevant. Later, French writers were to return to Dostoyevsky, but for other reasons.

From Germany and Italy only two voices were to be heard, those of Jünger and Moravia. The best or most famous, like Thomas Mann, had chosen exile. And it was an Italian in exile, Ignazio Silone, that the French discovered at this time, with his *Fontamara.*

Spain was similarly silent, except for a voice from the dead, that of Federico Garcia Lorca, who had been murdered in the Civil War.

Through the mediation of Gide and others, English novelists such as Conrad, Meredith, Galsworthy and D. H. Lawrence had enjoyed a considerable reputation. But this reputation had crumbled to the benefit of the all-powerful Irishman, James Joyce, whose star was now at its zenith. But then Joyce, who had lived in Italy, France and Switzerland, was more European than English. Only T. E. Lawrence, who was an outlaw and adventurer rather than a man of letters, and Virginia Woolf, were truly representative of the contemporary English novel in France.

The real discoveries came from the United States. Theodore Dreiser, Upton Sinclair, Sinclair Lewis and Sherwood Anderson had been translated, published and read. They also aroused curiosity. *Sanctuary*, prefaced by André Malraux, revealed William Faulkner, whose reputation in France spread back to his own country. Great interest was aroused by *42nd Parallel* and *Manhattan Transfer* by John Dos Passos, *A Farewell to Arms* by Ernest Hemingway, *God's Little Acre* and *Tobacco Road* by Erksine Caldwell and *Of Mice and Men* by John Steinbeck. While the French novelist despaired of himself and of his doomed civilization, the Americans revealed a new continent, new ways of looking at the human being and at the world. There were other subjects for fiction than the endless stories of love and heroism, other ways of treating character than endless psychological analysis. Taught by Malraux, Céline, Giono and Bernanos to pursue new ways, the younger French novelists were ready to assimilate this new influence.

The Americans helped them to rediscover life itself, sometimes in its more brutal, elementary forms: the world of modern, urban, industrial man, struggling against the limitations imposed upon his condition by society, the violence of his social and personal relationships and the frankness and audacity of his speech. This influence, it was realized, was not entirely new, and critics were not slow to point out the debt that the Americans in turn owed to Flaubert and the naturalists. But Hemingway, Dos Passos, Steinbeck and Faulkner brought air, light and water to the exhausted and almost moribund French novel. They helped it to renew its themes and its technique. Already, in *L'Etranger*, Camus had benefited from the lesson. The post-war novelists would be similarly affected.

Another, unexpected influence (from a solitary novelist, now dead, whose nationality had no great importance) was felt about this time, that of Kafka.

His most famous work, *The Trial*, published in France in 1933, passed unnoticed. In 1938, *The Castle* and *Metamorphosis* were published and received a great deal of attention. At first, Kafka was considered to be a fantastic, somewhat esoteric writer of fables, whose meaning remained obscure, but which were nevertheless impressive. In any case, they amazed and fascinated by the burning relevance of the questions asked by the writer of Prague some twenty or thirty years earlier. The hero of *The Trial* is also the man of 1938 about to be plunged into a war whose reasons he does not understand, who feels condemned, without appeal, by a trial at which he has not been present. *The Castle* is both the image of a society in which man is imprisoned as in a labyrinth and also a condition without hope. The foul creature into which Gregor Samsa changes in *The Metamorphosis* can as easily be one of humanity's own horrifying possibilities. Moreover, what one admires in Kafka, apart from the philosophical background, is the perfect credibility of each episode, the apparent calm of the narration and the utter readability of the story. His god, too, was Flaubert.

It was very largely from Kafka that French novelists were to borrow the philosophy of the absurd and a certain concept of literature by which, in attempting to transcend itself, it was transformed into something other than itself. Writing was to become not so much a matter of showing than of expressing, not so much of expressing as creating. The novel was to acquire more dignity. It was to pass from the rank of a means of expression to that of a work of art. Against the novel as understood by Kafka, Gide and Valéry could no longer have held the contemptuous reservations they expressed at the beginning of the century. Kafka salved the consciences of all those who were ambitious enough to follow in his footsteps.

Benefiting from these influences, the French novel proved bolder in the task of renewing its content and its techniques. It pursued two not always related and sometimes contradictory aims: to attain the dignity of a work of art and to make this work of art significant. The great novelists of every period and of every country were in agreement. However, after Benjamin Constant, Châteaubriand, Stendhal, Balzac and Flaubert, they had diverged into two camps: on the one side the believers in 'art for art's sake' and, on the other, those who sought to present 'a slice of life'. The first had rarely been novelists as such; the second were more concerned with truth than with beauty. The first wrote for a cultured *élite*, the second for the mass public. If a reconciliation was to come about, artists must be converted to the novel and novelists must adopt higher ambitions. The novel itself, that is, the novelists, must reconsider the powers and limitations of literature. It may be that the novel, in its traditional form, was doomed. Perhaps a new kind of novel would be born. Instead of being the normal mode of literature, perhaps it could appear in a form at once more noble and significant.

In the debate which opened around the subject of the novel, and its possible disappearance, the rudest blows were delivered by a man who claimed to be neither an artist not a novelist, but a philosopher: Jean-Paul Sartre. Nevertheless, Sartre did not wish to see the end of the novel, but a widening of its scope, its transformation. His work on the theory of the novel opened up tremendous possibilities.

Sartre, theoretician of the novel

Founding a kind of criticism that is philosophical as well as literary, Jean-Paul Sartre rejects categories and forms. He situates himself as a 'consciousness' confronted by another 'consciousness': that of the novelist. When he speaks of Faulkner, Dos Passos or François Mauriac, what interests him is what takes place in the consciousness of these novelists.

He first observes the existence of a special 'time' in the novel, a 'time' that is peculiar to each novelist, and which bears little relation to our own time. This observation is reminiscent of Bergson's discovery that real time is quite different to the time measured by clocks. The novelist constructs a past, present and future in order to deny 'man's misfortune of being temporal'. Whether he accelerates the passing of time or immobilizes it in a single moment, he deforms it. 'Most of the great contemporary authors, Proust, Joyce, Dos Passos, Faulkner, Gide, V. Woolf, have tried, each in his own way, to distort time. Some have deprived it of its past and future in order to reduce it to the pure intuition of the instant; others, like Dos Passos, have made of it a dead and closed memory, Proust and Faulkner have simply decapitated it. They have deprived it of its future, that is, the dimension of deeds and freedom.' This remark was to have considerable repercussions. Most of the young post-war novelists were to break with the traditional form of narrative and, going even further than James Joyce, who made the entire action of *Ulysses* take place in a single day, mixed past and future in the course of the same narrative, so as to capture and to show their characters in their totality, outside the arbitrary divisions of time. To the common observation according to which a man is never the same at different moments in time, Sartre adds another: the same man is also defined by the sum of his moments. For the compartmented and analytical view of the life of a character, Sartre substitutes a comprehensive, total view.

This view is not only that of the novelist; it is not an *a priori* of narrative. It is just as much the view adopted by the reader in the course of his reading as that of the writer in his writing. It is discovered by both as the novel proceeds, as the characters whose actions are described to us are born, live and die. Again, it is a question of the relationship between different consciousnesses: that of the reader, that of the writer and those of the fictional characters. For Jean-Paul Sartre, they are defined by their freedom. Perhaps it is not possible to place on the same plane both living characters (the novelist and the reader) and fictitious creations (the characters of the novel). But this is precisely why fictitious characters must give the illusion of being alive. They too are alive only when they exercise their freedom. In an important essay, Sartre reproaches Mauriac with treating his characters as if he were a creating, omniscient and omnipotent God, who knows in advance the answers to the questions he asks, whereas the novel should be an area in which these questions are resolved through the characters and situations. Not only does Mauriac pull the strings that make his characters move; he also speaks through their mouths. They are no more than a mask behind which he expresses himself. He has 'preferred' himself to them. It is only to be expected therefore that they do not surprise him, or us. Whereas a novel is written '*by* men and *for* men', M. Mauriac 'has chosen divine omniscience and omnipotence'. Conclusion: 'God is not an artist. Neither is M. Mauriac.'

This view of the novel, the novelist and their relationship within the 'self-making' work, and of the relationship between the novelist and the reader, who, in turn, 'makes' the novel (by the act of reading), was to have a deep and lasting influence upon later writers. These relationships being, by their very nature, ambiguous, the new novelists tried to reduce this ambiguity, either by an (admitted) excess of subjectivity, or by a punctilious objectivity. There appears, on the one hand, a 'literature of confession', in which the writer, taking himself as both the subject and object of his work, eschews any excursion into fiction, except in the simple 'arrangement' of the facts, and, on the other hand, a literature in which the writer wishes to exclude himself as much as possible from the work, leaving his story to unfold as if by its own internal power.

Whichever attitude the writer adopts, the novel gains in credibility and verisimilitude. The novelist himself assumes a seriousness that he has not always enjoyed. Those who would once have despised the novel as essentially unserious were obliged to take note of the 'novels' of Camus or of Sartre himself. Later, the belief even became current that these works constituted the most important (and least untruthful) branch of literature. They were regarded as a kind of code in which were expressed the anxieties of a whole period and the attempted solutions that the period offered. Sartre defined an attitude: that of the novelist to his work. He also claimed to be defining the content of the novel. If the novel had abandoned the study of types and characters (the miser, the spendthrift, the ambitious man, etc.), it should also renounce what Sartre calls 'essences' or 'natures'. There is no such thing, in his opinion, as the 'nature' of a lover, a betrayed husband, an ambitious man or a revolutionary; there is no such thing even as 'human nature'. It is meaningless therefore to speak of 'fate': a novel that purports to reveal the fate of a character substitutes for an objective view of an individual's life as it exists in society at a particular historical moment a metaphysical or religious view. This metaphysical view is, in turn, to be defined as part of a great system: that of the ruling class. This system has imposed upon the novelist, without him being aware of it, a philosophy of the world and a code of ethics which inevitably help to preserve the *status quo*. For immutable 'essences', that have been defined once and for all, Sartre substitutes 'existences', in which man, in total freedom, defines himself at each moment. The novel should depict infinitely varied 'situations', which are always new for the same individual and which demand from the man who lives them answers which are themselves always new and infinitely varied. To refer back to the example of Mauriac, Thérèse Desqueyroux is not a 'poisoner', but a woman who has used poison, that is, a woman who found herself in a situation that was such that she decided to act in the way she did. Similarly, there is no such thing as a 'lover', nor is there even an eternal 'love situation', defined once and for all. 'Essences' reduce action to schematic situations and individuals to stereotyped dummies. To consider man as an 'existence' thrown into a certain 'situation' on the contrary forces one to consider each event, each phenomenon, each individual reaction in its unique, localized truth. If the novel thus loses in verisimilitude (which itself is based upon mechanical logic), it gains in authenticity and becomes, for the writer himself, a discovery.

Maurice Blanchot

These views of Sartre are close to those of a critic who published a collection of articles at the beginning of the war: Maurice Blanchot. Instead of limiting the discussion to the novel, Blanchot enlarges it to include the whole of literature, that is, the art of writing itself. Writing is no more than a fabrication, albeit an artistic one. It is a kind of discipline by which the writer, without always wishing to, transforms himself, while at the same time transforming, at least ideally, the world. To be effective, this activity requires the complicity and collaboration of the reader. For the logical schema which places the producer in front of the consumer, Blanchot substitutes an 'existential' fact; the indissoluble synthesis in which the author, the work and the reader all participate. His only aim is to describe this synthesis phenomenologically.

Thus the search for new ways in the novel involves the search for new ways in criticism. The criteria by which works are judged, and which were based essentially on what the writer has created, are imperceptibly replaced by an examination of the author's intentions, by a description of the particular treatment he imposes upon the mysterious and always unique compound through which he enters the world and through which the world enters his work, by taking the bearings of the journey on which he sets out in search of a certain unknown territory. It is no longer a question of appreciating the value of a work. It is more a question of recognizing the country into which the work leads writer and reader, with both writing and reading functioning as a means of discovery. In the work of Maurice Blanchot, the critic is always accompanied by the philosopher and metaphysician. In his view, all writing, all language leads to silence. Writing is an apprenticeship to death. Some ten years later, certain writers (whom, like Samuel Beckett, one would scarcely call novelists at all) were to fulfil in a most striking way the theses enunciated by Maurice Blanchot.

In addition to this renewal in depth which was happening during the last few years before the war and which brought into question the novel and the whole of literature, certain minor changes in technique and form were to take place. Unconscious of the enormous developments that were later to affect them, the cinema and the radio made greater attempts to become media of artistic expression. In particular, the cinema, a medium *par excellence* of 'storytelling', strove to impart a certain style to its natural realism and to act upon the spectators' sensibility by means which were more and more its own. Sometimes it did so far more effectively than the novel. It was important, therefore, that the novel should find new methods of work. For certain of the new novelists, the 'story' itself lost all importance and was replaced by a study in depth that the cinema was unable to provide. Others adopted more or less overtly the cinema's narrative style and techniques of expression: the ellipse, the use of violent contrasts, the wandering eye of the camera. They wished to show that thought remained more agile than any images and was more capable than the cinema of moving in a world of allusion, allegory and symbol. In the competition which began between the narrative methods of the cinema and of the novel, the novel, in a refusal to admit defeat, became more and more ambitious in its aims. But it took whatever it could from the cinema.

The essential transformation which took place in the novel was none the less brought on by the approach of war. In face of war, and the threats which it involved, writing seemed a futile occupation if it did not result in a questioning of basic assumptions about the world and a deeper perception of the world, by which man, suddenly thrown off the rails of everyday life, might try (to some extent) to recover the control of which the independent course of events had deprived him. In the hubbub of events outside his control, he must weave the thread that would lead him out of the labyrinth. It was a propitious moment for the production of serious and significant works.

7 *Jean-Paul Sartre, Novelist*

Jean-Paul Sartre had already published a number of philosophical works when, in 1938, he made his début in literature with *La Nausée*. He was thirty-three; his original, very strongly expressed views on literature had for some time appeared in the columns of the *Nouvelle Revue Française*.

La Nausée is not so much a novel as a story with philosophical intentions. Its meaning is not immediately apparent and the author's intentions remain very largely obscure. But the reader cannot fail to respond to the very special world the author has created. It is a philosopher's world. It is also a novelist's world, hermetically sealed, in which various sorts of prisoners perform their dogged acts like blind men sunk in some sticky, viscous matter. The atmosphere is of the provincial *petite bourgeoisie*: conventional and stifling. Nothing ever happens: each act is smothered at birth by this sticky, enveloping mass. The hero of the story is a shy, indecisive, insignificant wretch, overwhelmed by his own life and by the lives of others, forever on the verge of disgust at the false appearances among which the mediocre ostentation of his miserable existence takes place. If he thinks of taking his own life, he discovers that even suicide would be meaningless. He feels out of place in a world that is already too full.

Roquentin commits an ideal act of revenge upon the world that has been imposed on him, on this existence which is his, but which he did not want. In describing his predicament, he cannot fail to observe its causes and to see through the appearances of the world that oppresses him. From this starting point, the author sets out on a philosophical, social, even political examination of a world that we gradually come to realize is in fact our own. It is not so much the world of self-interest as that of bad faith. A kind of tacit understanding has grown up between the *salauds* (swine), those who have found their place in society and who occupy it in all good conscience, and the vast mass formed by the victims of this society, by those who accept the established order that crushes them. Everybody, bourgeois and proletarian, exploiter and exploited, plays his part. And the play of which they are the unconscious actors continues in an atmosphere of extreme cordiality. But if one of the actors, like Roquentin, suddenly refuses to play and tries to look at it from the outside, the atmosphere is dissipated, appearances vanish to reveal the sordid bitterness of struggling animals. Underneath the smooth, polished surface of life, there is a void. Even the scenery is no more than scenery, that is to say, appearances.

The man who perceives the 'facticity' of the world, the unreality of the existence to which he is condemned, attempts to escape, into heaven, to God. But God proves deaf to his cries; the empty heavens send back to man the echo of his own words. No help can be expected from anyone. The individual is thrown back on himself, on his own consciousness, condemned to realize his freedom, to assume his condition. Abandoned by all, his only recourse is in this abandonment itself. All he can do is to explore its limits and become conscious of them. If he cannot find in them a basis for his lost dignity, at least he can find lucidity and authenticity.

In *La Nausée*, Roquentin accomplishes no more than the first part of this process: that of refusal. He discovers the world and to some extent discovers himself. He feels his own foreignness, his inadequacy. It is these feelings, plus a feeling of fundamental loneliness, that lead him to contemplate suicide. His rejection of the world, of others, of life, which is expressed by innumerable subtle forms of physical disgust, of nausea, condemns him to an even greater solitude: whether he leaves the world or stays in it makes no difference either way, and especially not to the world itself. If, in brief moments of illumination, he perceives his existence, it is only to fall ever more deeply into a 'facticity' that submerges and envelops him.

The short stories that form *Le Mur*, published in the following year, provide new illustrations of the philosophical positions Sartre had outlined in *La Nausée*. They are also better disguised, more successfully incarnated as literature. They beat more truly with the throb of the times. 'Le Mur', in which two Spanish revolutionaries are waiting to be shot, shows man in an extreme situation. This situation is assumed, conquered and overcome. The story distils, on the literary plane, all the horror of a tale by Edgar Allan Poe. Erostrate, in the story that bears his name, is Roquentin driven mad by an excess of lucidity. 'La Chambre' is about love transformed into total, impregnable solitude. The subject of 'L'Enfance d'un Chef' is bad faith at its extreme limit.

Sartrean Commitment

Sartre pursues his arguments to the point at which they become clear in themselves and accord with immediately perceptible common sense. Far from being unnecessary this détour disposes, one after another, of the foundations of evidence. Instead of shocking the reader into sudden agreement, Sartre invites him to collaborate with him in his search, to accompany him on his meandering way, to arrive with him in daylight: the way taken was the right one. This is not a mere philosopher's trick. It is by a series of such literary tricks that Sartre overcomes the resistance of the reader and finally has him in his power.

At the beginning of the war, Sartre was mobilized, captured by the Germans and then repatriated. During the war he published his most important philosophical work, *L'Etre et le Néant*, and wrote his first plays. His participation in the Resistance gave him at the liberation an intellectual authority of the first order. In 1945, he published the first volume of a series of novels called *Les Chemins de la Liberté*, in which he attempted to show the slow growth of consciousness more or less alienated in the struggles of the war and the Resistance. His philosophical ideas spread rapidly. In the blood-drenched atmosphere of post-war France, existentialism became fashionable, much as surrealism had done in the twenties. Disciples sprang up, and abroad people listened for the latest opinions to come from Saint-Germain-des-Prés. The newspapers were full of the discussion about 'commitment'.

Sartre, in effect, had no ambition to be a writer in the sense in which André Gide and Paul Valéry were writers. Like many others, he had been influenced by André Malraux, who, in fact, was scarcely older than himself. For Malraux, literature was one way of participating in the tragedy of the times. For years Sartre had resisted the political persuasions of Paul Nizan, but his years in the Resistance had revealed certain realities to him that had previously escaped the philosopher's attention. At the limit of this philosophy, whose essential principles he had learned from Heidegger and Husserl in pre-war Berlin, he discovered the necessity for action. If he refused to accept Marxism, whose philosophical foundations seemed to him to be insufficiently founded, he did not believe that existentialism could limit itself to a contemplation of the world or even an explanation of that world. Suddenly, to the astonishment of the readers of *La Nausée* (in which man was out of place in a world that was 'too full') and of *L'Etre et le Néant*, Sartre declared 'existentialism is a humanism'. The philosophical process must be extended into behaviour and be capable of establishing values and elaborating both an individual ethic and an ethic of man in society.

The commitment of the writer is one aspect of this ethic. It is one of the forms of that 'responsibility' that the philosopher has tacked on, as a logical necessity, to his theory of freedom. It means that the writer is not a high priest of art, that art for him is a way of expressing and transforming the world. The writer must be in the world, and from the various meanings that the world offers him, he must choose those that help humanity to become self-conscious, to change its destiny by increased knowledge and by a less fallible control over things.

The artist does not describe a play; he is an actor. What he says must contribute to the development of the whole, which should concern him and of which he is a part. The artist must be committed to his work – Sartre does not affirm that this philosophical commitment must necessarily lead to a social and political commitment. But such a commitment does almost follow from the premises, for how can the writer feel 'responsible' for himself, for others and for the progress of the world, and not in the end adopt a pragmatic attitude outside his work?

The idea of the 'responsibility' of the writer reappears in the presentation in 1945 of *Les Temps Modernes*. Once again, Sartre defines the nature of 'commitment' and explains it with the help of some striking examples: 'I hold Flaubert and Goncourt responsible for the repression that followed the Commune because they did not write a single line to prevent it.' Commitment, Sartre is saying, is not only moral or a matter of principle. It is not thought that commits, but action: for the writer, this means words. To remain silent, under whatever pretext, on any question whatever, is to refuse the writer's obligation to accept responsibility for the world; it is to maim that world and oneself.

By a philosophical détour, Sartre has rediscovered the 'mission' of the romantic poet, the bard of nature and the spokesman of mankind. His position is not far removed from that of the 'proletarian writers' of the thirties, for whom writing must serve to denounce the bourgeois world and aid in the emancipation of the exploited class. Sartre even uses the Marxist analysis, to the point of caricature, when he declares that Proust, in writing *A la Recherche du Temps Perdu,* 'chose to be a bourgeois . . . made himself the accomplice of bourgeois propaganda'.

Les Chemins de la Liberte

Sartre the novelist – this study is limited to examining this aspect of his prolific activity – attempted in *Les Chemins de la Liberté* to illustrate his philosophical theories and to provide an example of what the commitment of the writer should be.

Unfortunately, he came up against difficulties that he had not foreseen. These difficulties concern the working out of the novel itself and cast doubt on the correctness of the theory in practice. For if it is desirable that a novelist should be committed, he must first of all be a novelist. Lucidity, courage and intelligence are not enough. Is it not what they reveal of themselves, involuntarily and unconsciously, in their works, that makes a Dostoyevsky, a Balzac and a Dickens, and not, always, what they explicitly wished to say? Sartre's plan in *Les Chemins de la Liberté* is so visible as to prevent the appearance of those shadowy regions in which beings evolve, of which perhaps they are made and by which they are a constant source of surprise and evade the most subtle methods of investigation. In his criticism of François Mauriac, Sartre had suggested the ways the novel should take so as not to substitute intellectual abstraction for life and the personality of the novelist for living people. Then, in his own work, he fell into mistakes which were not exactly the ones he had condemned, but perhaps worse. Turning the full lights on to his characters, he produces flat images compensating for their superficiality by a mechanical complexity that leaves the cogs showing. Our minds may be interested but our hearts remain unmoved. In the end, Sartre realized his own failure and abandoned the project before its completion. The structure that he had built in three stages–*L'Age de Raison, Le Sursis, La Mort dans l'Ame*–remains without a roof. Since then, it has suffered a great deal at the hands of the elements.

L'Age de Raison shows young people discovering life in a world about to be plunged into war. Almost in spite of themselves, they feel the weight of the times on their shoulders. But their problems are none the less strictly personal. They confront them with all the clumsiness and misplaced enthusiasm of youth. Even Mathieu, the oldest of them, asks himself some surprising questions, such as whether it is morally permissible to arrange for one's mistress to have an abortion. It is only too obvious that the question has been asked in order to provide material for long discussions that are of interest only to the author. Not one of them succeeds in formulating the problems that one would expect him to be interested in, or really becomes conscious of his responsibilities, without endless, abstract discussion. *L'Age de Raison* is less reminiscent of Sartre's *Nausée* than of the Gide of *Les Caves du Vatican* (especially the parts in which Lafcadio appears) or of *Les Faux Monnayeurs* (with its criss-cross of feelings, gratuitous acts and emotional dramas also largely gratuitous). Sartre seems to limit himself to exploiting the possibilities of the Gidean universe, even if he does pursue it to its limit, and is scarcely concerned at all with moral or religious problems.

In *Le Sursis,* his ambitions are greater and the technique of composition more original. Obsessed by Dos Passos (whom he has called 'the greatest writer of our time'), Sartre tries to give a complete view of the world preparing for war during the respite accorded by the Munich agreements. He uses the techniques that served Dos Passos in *1919* and *42nd Parallel*: confusion of time and place, simultaneity of individual and social events, the introduction of historical characters, the mixing of the historical and the fictional. The result is a big, smoothly-running machine that does credit to the writer's virtuosity. Unfortunately, it evokes in the reader no more than an intellectual excitement. In the hubbub of events, characters and feelings, no single character makes much impression on us, and everything the writer has painfully taught us we already knew from the newspapers. Sartre is only at the second stage of his demonstration. Perhaps what he wanted to show was that in our dramatic times the individual has been submerged by society almost to the point of losing his separate identity.

In *La Mort dans l'Ame*, we find once more the Mathieu of *L'Age de Raison,* now mobilized, a soldier despite himself and contrary to his moral and political convictions. Like one of Malraux's heroes, he participates in war 'without having any liking for it'. But he is not content to be a cog in a machine. He makes it a point of honour to prepare and reflect on every act he performs. He realizes that the war he is engaged in fighting is a 'false war' and that he is himself no more than a paper soldier. Everything collapses even before he has had time to believe in what he was doing. Capitulation follows defeat.

The next volume was to show us Mathieu becoming conscious, through the collective destiny of a whole people, of problems that concerned himself alone. In resolving them he would at last succeed in assuming his 'freedom'.

Sartre's experiment in fiction ends in failure, but his failure is worth more than many a success. Despite its didactic aims, it remains a true and comprehensive account of a period, of the spiritual, moral and intellectual itinerary of a section of the French intelligentsia. The questions that Mathieu asked himself, and no doubt that Sartre asked himself, are placed in their context and developed in their true light. They are examined with seriousness, in all their implications. We see how men, swamped by society, helpless amid events outside their control, achieve a sense of responsibility that is not so much philosophical as human and how the individual is formed by successive victories in the course of constant challenge. If, among other things, Sartre tried to show that there was no such thing as 'human nature', that there are as many reactions to a situation as there are people and that it would be a failure of courage to sink into any one of them, then he has succeeded. The ethic that Sartre has chosen not to develop in a separate treatise finds a practical application throughout these novels. One is amazed at the bad faith of those who have reproached Sartre with wishing to 'debase man'. His intention and his achievement indicate the exact opposite.

This failure in the field of the novel provides another obvious lesson: one cannot suddenly decide to become a novelist. Words cannot be written by the exercise of demonstrative reason. All the qualities one may possess in other fields are perversely transformed into defects when one wishes to use them as a poet and not as a philosopher. The fictional world that Sartre carries within him has found its expression in his plays, not in *Les Chemins de la Liberté*. For in the theatre the writer must express himself by simpler means. The doors of meaning must be opened, even if they have to be forced open: the movement of drama can contain and disguise that of logical demonstration. It is unlikely that Sartre will take up the novel again. It is certain, however, that he benefited as a writer from his ambitious and honourable failure.

8 *Albert Camus, Novelist*

The literary importance of Albert Camus, and his influence and reputation as a moralist and philosopher are as great as those of Jean-Paul Sartre. Like Sartre, Camus cannot be considered simply as a novelist; like Sartre, he found expression both in the theatre and in the essay; and like Sartre, he played and still plays the role of a spiritual advisor. His sudden death, at a time when he had just attained the eminence of the Nobel Prize and had so much more to say, crowned his work with a halo of tragedy.

He began his literary career in Algiers, before the war, with two short works, written under the influence of Gide, which seem bathed in the strong, clear light of his Mediterranean homeland: *L'Envers et l'Endroit*, 1937, and *Noces*, 1938. He showed himself to be a poet and a stylist, eloquent, lyrical and serious, who possessed a strong feeling for nature and an equally strong desire for happiness, which his conscience already condemned as self-indulgence. *L'Etranger*, published in 1942, suddenly made him famous. This novel was followed almost at once by *Le Mythe de Sisyphe*, in which he expressed a conception of the world which became popular at once under the name of 'the philosophy of the absurd'. Both works are profoundly in tune with the period: it is easy to see in them a reflection of the desperate state in which the man of that time found himself, a sleepwalker in the midst of events quite outside his control. The name of Camus became linked with that of Sartre. They became the twin champions of new ways of feeling and thinking, of what is called, but which was not yet known as such, 'existentialism'. In fact, these two newcomers, each of major importance, could hardly be farther removed from each other, both as thinkers and as writers. It needed the spectacular quarrel of 1952 for this to be made apparent to everybody.

In *L'Etranger*, Camus borrowed the narrative techniques and to some extent the style of such American novelists as Hemingway. The novelist himself remains objective; he refrains from intervening in the fate of his characters, from using them as mouthpieces for himself and from making explicit their thoughts and feelings. He limits himself to describing the actions and gestures of his hero, Meursault, to noting the phases of his behaviour within the Behaviourist discipline. Meursault does not 'exist'; he merely reacts to the impulses he receives. His mother's death elicits no expression of feeling on his part: he has nothing to say about it. He becomes a murderer because of a beach, an Arab, the sun, a revolver in his pocket – a combination of circumstances that he has neither sought nor desired. He attends his own trial, without feeling in the least concerned by the cross-examination, the speeches of prosecution and defence, the picture that is built up of him, or even by the verdict itself. He walks to the guillotine without a word, as if it was not he who was about to be executed.

Guilty of murder? What is murder? What does guilty mean? Everything points to him as a victim of anonymous forces which conspire to bring about his downfall. He stumbled against them and they destroyed him. His death has no more meaning than his birth or his life. He was born into an indifferent world; the world rejected him with the same indifference. He was never 'in the world'. He never 'lived'.

The work bore no allegory, no symbol. How could the reader be satisfied with the literalness of the narrative? How could he avoid looking for the author's intentions? Or avoid trying to see himself in Meursault. Because of the quasi-anonymity of this unusual hero, any reader during the years of the occupation could slip into the skin of this character, compare his own fate, his own story with the sad freak described in the book. The author used his colours to paint a general, social situation; the lighting he used was valid for each indivudual. Similarly, the unformulated ethic of the story corroborated the philosophical perceptions of *Le Mythe de Sisyphe*, which, in the novel, were written down in black and white. They were an invitation to think of the world in terms of the 'absurd' and life in terms of despair. This is what Camus meant by his 'outsider'. In the essay he declares that he wants to imagine Sisyphus 'happy', that he must be imagined as such. The absurd task to which Sisyphus is condemned would lead one to think the opposite. Happiness is a trap; life too is a trap. *L'Etranger* provided a cruel, but seemingly true image of the human condition.

The attitude of Albert Camus the man corrected this image. He was not despairing, since he participated in the Resistance. The Liberation, by means of the newspaper of which he was editor, even made him the intellectual master of certain disorientated sections of public opinion, the spiritual master of a new generation. Each day he preached courage, lucidity, a will to face facts, a certain kind of Stoicism. Far from resigning himself to despair, he announced rather too early the imminent end of nihilism and the arrival of a new kind of hope. He had no wish to be among the destroyers, but among the rebuilders; without moralizing, he appeared as a moralist.

In 1946, he gave up journalism to devote himself to his literary work.

In 1947, he published *La Peste*, which enjoyed a spectacular success.

This work is even less a novel than *L'Etranger*. It is a chronicle, inspired by Daniel Defoe's *Journal of the Plague Year,* which tells of an imaginary epidemic at Oran in Algeria at some unspecified time. Camus spares no pains in his description of the scourge, but at no point does he indulge in melodramatic effects for their own sake.

One realizes quite early on that the story is to be understood at different levels at once, that the description is an excuse for a lesson. The story this time is an allegory. Events, the actions of the characters (even the choice of characters), their thoughts and feelings reflect events, actions, thoughts and feelings that the reader has known or shared. The plague is an image of fascism, of the occupation. Like a plague, fascism contaminated a whole people, most of Europe and a large section of the French nation, victims or accomplices. 'Everybody carries the plague within himself . . .' The lesson is as much one of social morality as of personal morality. To combat the disease it is not enough to consult specialists (doctors) who are armed for the struggle. Everyone must fight it within himself, if he is to be saved.

The characters presented by Camus behave like most men placed in an extraordinary situation. Rieux, lucid and generous, having no illusions about his abilities (and closest probably to the thoughts and feelings of the author), acts as an example to others: identifying himself with the victims, he defends the imperatives of charity carried to the point of sacrifice. He envisages a 'sanctity without God' (he is an agnostic) which seems to him to be 'the only concrete problem' to resolve. Salvation through God has become impossible, so salvation through man must take its place. However abject the victims became, however consenting and contagious, they never deserved their fate. Whatever the degree of their responsibility, they represented the only concrete reality in which other more lucid, less selfish men could interest themselves. Misery brings men together. It is together that they should bring about their salvation.

The lesson is no longer that of *L'Etranger*. The accent is still placed upon the absurdity of the world and of the human condition, on the eternal denial of justice to man. But he no longer answers this by the indifference of Meursault. He believes in the possibility of solutions, general and particular. Life continues to be devoid of meaning; man acquires nobility and dignity in living it. Altruism is added to solitary Stoicism.

The admirers of *L'Etranger* were surprised by what they took to be a reversal of philosophical positions. New admirers were not wanting, people who found satisfaction in this 'lay sanctity' or, as it was rather cruelly described, 'this boy-scout morality'. It seemed that Camus had abandoned the revolt that he had preached and allied himself rather too quickly with the band of tormented but ineffectual 'good souls'.

Both had used Camus for their own ends, taking only what would serve their own cause. In fact, from his first writings, from *L'Envers et l'Endroit*, which one must always refer back to if one is to understand him, Camus strove to reconcile contradictory but equally vital tendencies in himself: the love of life and the search for happiness, the absurdity of the human condition and the impossibility of happiness.

He explained himself openly in *L'Homme Révolté*, 1951, an essay which would not concern us here were it not that it throws light on the intentions of the novelist.

It is a long deposition against History, whom men have made into a demanding mistress whose every whim they are quite willing to satisfy and in whom they hope to find a necessary and sufficient reason for their actions. It is also a deposition, more or less documented (though sometimes, one feels, at second hand), against those powerful individuals who, in the course of History, either in their literary, philosophical or political work, have taken as their starting-point this deep-rooted feeling of 'revolt' that Camus sees in every man. They have to a greater or lesser degree departed from this 'revolt' in the interests of their selfish, arrogant work. Whether they be de Sade, Lautréamont or Rimbaud, Marx or Lenin, they have corrupted and perverted 'revolt' and arrived at monstrous systems: throughout the centuries they have each contributed to the progressive enslavement of humanity. While wanting men to be more lucid, more free, more happy, they have added to their confusion and misery. Camus turns away from these power-drunk geniuses and contrasts them with the Greek, Mediterranean genius, compounded of confidence in man, reason, life, content to resolve problems that are within its reach. The harsh Mediterranean sunlight must dissipate the misty miasmas of diseased imaginations.

The work is disappointing – in its analyses, more so in its conclusion. Putting an end at last to all equivocation, Camus gained a public that was only too ready for an intellectually respectable justification of its own conservatism and antipathy to change. Camus put their consciences to rest, provided them with arguments and made himself 'acceptable', even if he preached lessons that were difficult to live up to. Mediterranean wisdom was inadequate in dealing with the problems that humanity would have to solve if it was to enter without too much pain into the nuclear age. This revolt against History, this spirited return to reasonable but somewhat extenuated values sounded more like an abrogation of responsibility than an appeal for progress.

As a result of *L'Homme Révolté*, Camus quarrelled with Breton, with the literary avant-garde (to whom he was quite indifferent) and more seriously with Sartre. In his 'letter to Albert Camus', Sartre called upon the author of *L'Homme Révolté* to assume his responsibilities, to delcare openly what side he was on. He categorized Camus, none too subtly, as a 'liberal' thinker in the midst of a decadent bourgeoisie attached to its privileges. Camus's reply displays the quiet dignity of the artist, of the man who refrains from drawing conclusions for fear of adding to the 'tyranny of ideologies'. The arguments he put forward were not ones to convince Sartre any more than the admirers of *L'Etranger*. In fact Sartre and Camus no longer spoke a common language and it is not easy to say which of the two remained more faithful to himself.

After this outburtst, Albert Camus concerned himself less and less with political and social problems and sought to deepen the material of his art. As a '*pied noir*', or native of Algeria, he was expected to take sides in the war that was ravaging his country. Instead, he let it be known that in a conflict that raged not only in his country but in himself he had no intention of deciding who was right and who was wrong.

In 1956 he published *La Chute*, which was generally acclaimed as his best work. In it he gave greater play to ambiguity than ever before. A *salaud* (in the Sartrean sense of the term) reveals his motives, finding innumerable reasons for justifying his cowardly and cynical conduct. He would not appear to have anything in common with the author. Could certain of his characteristics, many of his dislikes and attitudes of mind be those of Camus, or indeed ours? Is this a case for the defence or the prosecution? Is he guilty? Or a victim? Should he be condemned or acquitted? These questions are left unanswered.

No doubt the author did not wish it otherwise. Tired of playing the role of spiritual counsellor, he hoped that the reader would judge him by his art. If he acts as a witness, he does so in the way that Dostoyevsky does in *Notes from the Underworld*. It is once more a case for a refusal of History and ideologies, or 'totalitarian' man, for a moral discipline which seems to be above the capacities of our period and our minds.

The stories in *L'Exil et le Royaume*, 1957, accentuate the choice in favour of art and style which makes each of them an accomplished 'uncommitted' work. It was at this time that the Swedish Academy made this forty-four-year-old writer the youngest recipient of the Nobel Prize and the young laureate made a speech for the occasion which alienated a large part of the left-wing intelligentsia. Two years later he was killed in a car crash. The entire world paid him homage.

The philosophical and literary development of Albert Camus, which always sprang from the noblest of motives, was concealed behind the warm, open, generous nature of the man: *La Chute* and *L'Etranger* were not separated by an abyss. The literary and artistic integrity that is apparent in *L'Exil et le Royaume* was already there in *L'Envers et l'Endroit* and even more so in *Noces*. It would be odd indeed to reproach a writer with wishing to be an artist.

It would be true to say that in the same man the artist cohabited with the thinker, the moralist and the man of action. People have tried to limit him to one or other aspect of his complex personality and make him stick to it, whereas he gave voice alternately to each of the conflicting tendencies within him and, in a tense and moving effort tried to reconcile them.

In striving after an impossible harmony, a unity that he so much desired, his literary genius was nourished on contradiction. It needed courage on the part of a man so doubtful of his own wisdom to refuse to play the role of sage that a period avid for faith and certitude had unconsciously thrust upon him. He remains a witness of that period, striving to place his work above its changing moods, so as better to express its more permanent aspects. The search for art was for him a search for eternity.

9 *Existentialism and its Influence*

The ways opened by Sartre and Camus during and just before the war were followed with enthusiasm by younger novelists once the war was over. The events experienced, the sufferings endured, the boredom, the disgust, the absence of individual and collective prospects, the feeling that 'victory' had been turned into one great mess were more than sufficient to foster a general attitude of 'what's the use?' and corroborated the philosophical premises of Sartre concerning the world of *salauds* motivated by *mauvaise foi* ('bad faith') and the conclusions of Camus on 'the absurd'. The fashion was for the *roman noir*, the 'black novel'. Despair was worn like a badge; the heroes formed an imposing collection of cowards and failures. One even went so far as to speak of an 'existentialist school' which, out of a taste for symmetry, was compared with surrealism after the First World War. A type of 'Sartrean novel' was thought to exist, a novel of extraordinary situations in which man revealed himself under the aspects of cowardice, fear, dishonesty and protested more or less overtly against the universal denial of justice of which he was a victim. Some young novelists found an additional confirmation of their philosophy of 'abandon' in the concomitant support brought by the *romanciers de l'aveu* and, curiously enough, the neo-realism of the Italian writers and film directors.

If an 'existentialist school' never really existed, it is true none the less that certain tendencies were shared by the new novelists of the immediate post-war years and, although their works were very different, a certain type of novel emerged from pre-war practice. It was as near as possible to documentary and confession. There was an attempt to separate oneself as much as possible from what might be called 'literature': a concern for construction and verisimilitude, the preoccupation with being a 'writer' and 'artist', at the expense of what was called 'the authentic', and which, even in the exceptional or pathological should give an impression of the naked truth as really experienced. The objective was not so much to create as to express, to communicate. The quality of the communication was of secondary importance. It was enough that it existed and established the reality of the living person, broke through his solitude, even if this solitude addressed itself only to other solitudes. And, in fact, communication is more likely to be effected at the physical and conscious levels than at that of values (destroyed or largely damaged by the war) or art (an occupation for the indolent aesthete). When all seemed lost, there still remained the elementary world of instinct and impulse in which we live. With relentless lucidity, the 'existentialist novel' stripped souls and bodies bare. It made them neither more beautiful, nor more likable. They were no doubt more true. Perhaps because of it we obtained a truer picture of man.

To the influence of the American novel, of Kafka, of the cinema others were added which helped to make up the prevailing 'atmosphere' of the post-war French novel. The Marquis de Sade, an outcast imprisoned in the hell of private libraries, became suddenly fashionable. Serious studies of his work began to appear (by Paulhan, Bataille, Blanchot, Simone de Beauvoir) and publishers risked editions of his works. After a century and a half, the strength of public condemnation was such that the state intervened and the works returned to their former clandestine existence. Henry Miller, a contemporary American novelist, was similarly treated: his *Tropic of Cancer*, already banned in the United States, had the effect of a bombshell. Again, the Law intervened, prosecuted his translators and publishers, but faced with the protests of writers and critics gave up the struggle. Never more than at that time was it felt that literature was capable of breaking its bonds. The novel particularly was apt to say everything, to show everything: no region of man's activity, feelings and thoughts (even what might be considered impossible to admit) seemed able to escape being expressed. It was thought that there was virtue in scandal, that one should carry it to the point at which all defences, taboos and prohibitions should be lifted, to reveal man free, true and responsible. Since the social revolution had failed and seemed to recede more and more into the future, one could at least effect a revolution in morals.

Simone de Beavoir

Among the novelists – Mouloudji, Boris Vian, Colette Audry, Marguerite Duras, Jacques-Laurent Bost and many others – whose names have recurred in the pages of *Temps Modernes*, Simone de Beauvoir has certainly been one of the most gifted and tenacious. A friend of Sartre and like him a teacher for many years in lycée and university, she shares his philosophical views. These she has presented in two theoretical works, *Pyrrhus et Cinéas*, 1944, and *Pour une Morale de l'Ambiguïté*, 1947.

Her first book was a novel, *L'Invitée*, published in 1943, and it brought her immediate fame. In it the author dispensed with psychological analysis and showed different characters in 'situations'. Caring nothing either for morals or for the conformism that novelists (male and female) generally demonstrate in the portrayal of their heroines, Simone de Beauvoir presented women, in their everyday behaviour and dealing with the most serious problems, that one had not yet met in fiction. Françoise displays the usual desire for happiness and security that are generally attributed to her sex, but she cannot conceal her wish to affirm herself as an independent, free human being. Xavière, whom she has 'invited' to live with her in her pseudo-home, could stand as the type of the existentialist hero that we shall often see recreated later. A girl liberated from bourgeois conformity, she is also liberated from dependence on anything at all: she lives according to her instincts, in the immediacy of the moment; without even being aware of it, she tramples on all rules of social life and even of manners. Françoise admires her, but at the same time cannot bear her. She sees her as an oppressive 'consciousness' who tyrannizes her own consciousness. Later, Sartre was to say 'Hell is other people'.

The novels which follow – *Le Sang des Autres*, 1944, *Tous les Hommes sont Mortels*, 1947 – are not based on the same 'lived' (or living) experience and reveal to a greater degree their philosophical strings. *Le Sang des Autres* treats the problem of responsibility through the medium of an episode of the Resistance: the leader of a network reflects upon his moral right to send men to their deaths. He chooses to accept his mission even when he realizes that he is responsible for the death of the woman he loves. *Tous les Hommes sont mortels* takes up, in the form of a philosophical allegory, the old dream of immortality which rests in the heart of every individual. The author concludes that death is an intrinsic part of our destiny. It is only in *Les Mandarins* that Simone de Beauvoir rediscovers the fictional vein of *L'Invitée.*

The subject of *Les Mandarins* is mainly the left-wing intellectuals (one can recognize Sartre and Camus) and, in the form of a history of the immediate post-war years, the problem of commitment. Can an intellectual, in all conscience, limit himself to being no more than an intellectual? If he throws himself into political action and, for example, becomes a Communist, can he still claim to be an intellectual? Rather than answering these questions as a philosopher or moralist, Simone de Beauvoir answers them as a novelist, by depicting behaviour that illustrates certain attitudes to life. One of her heroes chooses political action: because of circumstances he goes from disillusion to disillusion. Another chooses to represent the conscience (truth before all, whatever the political results may be): in order to save a woman he loves, he finds himself condemned to perjury. Both wished to take on the problems of their time and fulfil the role that their intellectual's conscience dictated. Both failed. All that was left to them was to accept the condition of the 'mandarin': an intellectual reduced to the functions and limitations of writing.

This sincere, passionate work describes the deceptions of the post-war left-wing intelligentsia. The author is not, of course, advocating an abandonment or refusal of commitment, but trying rather to draw the limits of this commitment. For her, accepting the condition of being an intellectual means refusing to consider this condition as 'given', but on the contrary to create it at every moment through choice and the exercise of responsibility. It thus resembles, together with some additional powers, the condition of every human being: it is not so much a matter of selecting among a number of possibilities as cutting one's own way through a forest of ambiguities. This view is a moral and philosophical one. It touches upon the novel in so far as life erupts into the play of ideas. More successfully than in her two preceding novels, Simone de Beauvoir managed to mix them in the right proportions. The destiny of each character springs from a lived experience.

As in the work of Sartre, the desire to edify (in the best sense of the word) is not absent from the novelist's intentions. Existentialist novelists wish to write works that 'signify' something rather than 'significant' ones. In less gifted hands this resulted in a more or less well-ordered, lifeless and somewhat dated ballet of philosophical, moral or even sociological concepts. Such works have historical value: they help us to recreate that confused period in our recent history. In writing *Mémoires d'une Jeune Fille Rangée*, 1958, followed by *La Force de l'Age* (which for the war and occupation are openly in the form of a journal), the author of *Le Deuxième Sexe* shows her preference for autobiography and the direct account over the fictional form. The necessities of invention can no longer distort what she feels, in all honesty, should be told.

Jean Genet

Jean Genet belongs to no school and owes nothing to existentialist precepts. Nevertheless, he represented for Sartre such a brilliant example of what a writer could and should be according to the philosopher's conception of literature, he fulfilled so completely the conditions that Sarte was appealing for, that he might be considered as a distant relation of the existentialist family.

Genet is an outlaw, both as a writer and as a man, thrown from birth into the depths of a society that treated him as garbage. An orphan, a juvenile delinquent who spent his adolescence in various remand homes, a thief condemned to prison, a homosexual exhibitionist, an apologist for perjury and informing, he accepts his rejection by society. In *Saint Genet, Comédien et Martyr*, Sartre shows brilliantly how his hero deliberately chose to incarnate evil and how, in choosing it, he became, with admirable literary results, its inspired bard.

Even in his novels – *Notre Dame des Fleurs*, *Miracle de la Rose*, *Pompes Funèbres*, Genet is in fact more a poet than a novelist. His language is rich, ceremonial and hieratic; it transfigures, purifies the filth in which he wallows. Whether the subject of his song is humiliation (which has free rein in prisons and borstals), homosexuality (which he voluntarily accepts as a vice), the beauties of robbery, or the spiritual pleasures that accrue to the informer or criminal, his song rises, paradoxically, to a strong, pure flame. The word 'sanctity' ('sanctity is my aim . . . I want all my actions to lead me to that state that I have never known') neither shocks us nor makes us smile, even if one realizes that it is the sanctity of evil. Setting out to 'name reputedly shameful feelings with words that are usually reserved for noble sentiments', he succeeds in making theft seem courageous, betrayal holy and magnificent and crime heroic. For Genet the homosexual, 'evil is virility'. It is this evil that is the object of his tragic pursuit, a pursuit that remains unfulfilled except through the sexual act. Far from being a rebel, he prefers to remain a victim. His desire is that the world, 'with its admirable structure of laws', should crush him.

His language is particularly theatrical. It is not my business here to deal with this aspect of his literary work. None the less, it should be noted that the ambiguity of his characters – and of the writer – that is revealed in *Les Bonnes, Les Nègres* and *Le Balcon* finds a more satisfying expression in the theatre, where the vast 'illusion' of the world finds an equivalent illusion in a vast and subtle play of mirrors.

The 'maids' play the roles of their mistresses; the 'blacks' disguise themselves as whites; in *Le Balcon* respectable characters in a house of illusions act out, by means of disguise and parody, the great roles that they would like to play in real life. For Genet, man is at once what he is and what he wishes to appear. He finds greater satisfaction in appearance than in being, or, to go further, appearance *is* being. Other ambiguities strengthen and illustrate this fundamental ambiguity of a game that is confused with reality. And this play within a play gives illusion the stuff of truth, lends to Genet's plays a metaphysical depth that is not apparent in his novels, which are usually too close to personal experience. The poet of evil acquires in his plays the dimensions of a perceptive observer of morals, a diviner and an explorer. If his plays are no less scandalous than his other work, it is not because of a facile, generalized inversion of values, but rather by the revelation of some hidden, fundamental region of the unconscious. Life is a comedy that man plays to himself. One can laugh at seeing him fall for his own deceptions, but when it becomes clear that he is not the dupe of his actions or his fantasies, and yet cannot live without his illusions, the comedy takes on a tragic power which forces us to turn our attention upon ourselves. In spite of himself, the poet of evil changes into a moralist. In the last resort, the only certain reality that he places before our eyes is death, the state in which, as Sartre would say, the *en-soi* ('in-itself') merges into the *pour-soi* ('for-itself').

Raymond Guérin

Existentialism has been reproached for its merciless view of man. It has sometimes been accused of over-emphasizing our physiological behaviour. In this field, Sartre and his disciples were to be rapidly overtaken. For Raymond Guérin, who had written and published before Sartre and is therefore in no sense his disciple, physiology became an obsession. But it is doubtful whether he would have pursued it to the same extent if the climate created by existentialism had not already existed.

After a traditional novel, published before the war, Raymond Guérin produced, in 1941, *Quand vient la Fin*. The main character is the father of the narrator. He dies of cancer of the anus, and the entire novel is devoted to a long narration of the agony. *L'Apprenti*, 1946, a disguised autobiography, concerns an adolescence which is obsessed by anxieties less of a moral or metaphysical nature than physiological; it describes in great detail the compulsive habit of masturbation. *La Confession de Diogène*, 1948, reconstructs the life of the ancient philosopher as a contemporary novelist might see him: profoundly anarchistic, he despises honours, wealth and fame, and disdains everything that gives man the illusion of controlling events by knowledge or of surmounting his condition by religions, philosophies or ethical systems. Diogenes is not a rebel. He feels no desire to reform the lives of his contemporaries. He wishes to be no more than a 'humble observer of the human condition'. He seeks his own happiness outside society and events. In *La Main Passe* we are invited to read of the adventures of a modern Diogenes. The satire is more bitter, the anti-conformism more virulent, the language more explosive. 'Scandalous' scenes and observations that might be considered repugnant abound. The hero of the novel, Patrick Beaurepaire, affirms that one should not try to escape the physiological: 'The creature is no more than the viscera that motivate him . . . The best men behave as if they had the entrails of swine and snouts that love to poke into the filthiest orifices . . .' There is no other reality behind love; the practice of the domestic virtues, the exercise of thought are no more than the egoism of needs and the means capable of satisfying them. There is, in fact, no other existence than that of an insatiable body which, in order to survive and maintain itself in a state of relative equilibrium, smells out and swallows whatever it needs. For Raymond Guérin, the explanation of man and of the world, of their vain, age-old agitations is not difficult to find, if one so wishes, at the lowest level. All the rest is illusion and, he adds, a dangerous illusion that prevents us from living. If we wish to found a system based on wisdom, we must start from 'human stupidity', with its moods and viscera. Beside this radical philosophy, the ethical complexities of existentialism seem to spring from an incurable idealism.

In *Parmi tant d'autres Feux*, 1949, Raymond Guérin returns to the character of *L'Apprenti*, Monsieur Hermès, and plunges him into life. What he finds is disillusion of every kind, in mediocrity, blindness, the machinations of fate and of others against his own poor life. He loves a woman, but never finds love. He marries another. She introduces him into a mean, bourgeois milieu and then dies of tuberculosis. Leaving the provinces for Paris, where he hopes to become a writer, he comes up against all the fashionable social myths: love and money, art and death. He finds it impossible to be simply a man of good will. He finds again the woman he first loved, but is not sure that she will bring him happiness. He remains an eternal 'apprentice'. *Les Poulpes*, 1953, brings the writer's work to an end. He presents it as 'a book of utter derision, derisory even in its most immediate inspiration'.

With his rough, bitter, satirical talent, an enemy of all the graces of writing, Raymond Guérin went straight to what he wanted to say, eschewing all decoration, but leaving none the less a bitter scent of poetry in his hyper-realistic descriptions. There is in his work one thing of value to which he sacrified all else – expression.

By bringing into the 'existentialist' fold two writers who in no way claimed to belong to it, we have shown that this school has not been particularly rich in novelists of value: five or six promising talents that are now forgotten. They were soon attracted to other activities, their fiction proving to be no more than a transitional stage to other forms of expression.

On the other hand, Sartre's philosophical theories and his critique of the traditional novel influenced to a greater or lesser degree most young novelists up to 1950. Sartre helped them to become self-conscious, taught them to use themselves as instruments, supplied them with a view of the world and a care for language that was more direct and less superficial than the 'narrative' cultivated by their elders. He helped some of them, who were later to find their own voices, to discover their talents more quickly, more surely and more confidently, even though they had not long since emerged from the 'existentialist' atmosphere and were not always ready to acknowledge its influence.

In 1946, in a collection edited by Albert Camus, Colette Audry published some short stories that were dedicated to Jean-Paul Sartre, *On joue pendant*. These stories depicted characters whose lives were generally tragic, in spite of the fact that their sincerity and courage should have turned them rather to some form of happiness and taste for life. After the childhood memories of *Aux Yeux du Souvenir*, 1947, she remained silent until 1962. *Derrière la Baignoire* tells the story of a dog and its owner and of their affectionate, though sometimes troubled relationship. It is a moving, simply-written story, but outside anything that might be called literature.

There is the same simplicity of tone and expression in the work of Roger Grenier, accompanied by an element of humour, a love of the strange, and an apparently unemotional involvement in people's personal dramas: *Les Embuscades*, which relates a number of marginal episodes in the Resistance, and *La Voie Romaine*, which concerns the lives of the unillusioned youth of the immediate post-war years. Roger Grenier is a perceptive and able storyteller. His first stories were published in *Les Temps Modernes*.

Marguerite Duras, who has recently enjoyed considerable success in the cinema, also published 'existentialist' stories in Sartre's review before establishing herself with *Un Barrage contre le Pacifique* (based on childhood memories), *Les Petits Chevaux de Tarquinia*, *Moderato Cantabile* and *Le Square*. She wishes to be neither a philosopher nor a moralist. A dialectic of presence and absence, silence and words, life and death is apparent in these admirably constructed stories which seem to have no other ambition than to show life as it is, full of indefinable mysteries, a thick network of relationships that people weave between themselves. Marguerite Duras could take an honourable place in the 'new novel' with works like *Dix Heures du Soir en Eté* and *L'Après-midi de M. Andesmas*.

Jean Cau, who was for a long time Sartre's secretary, tried to find his own voice in a number of semi-humorous, semi-satirical works before writing in *Les Paroissiens,* 1958, a kind of *éducation sentimentale* for his generation – or that section of it that meets beneath the tower of Saint-Germain-des-Prés. *La Pitié de Dieu*, 1961, is a more ambitious work, written in a spirit closer to Genet than Sartre, and is executed with confidence and brilliance.

10 *Tradition and Innovation*

Side by side with the existentialist current of thought, historians of ideas have distinguished, in post-war France, a personalist current represented by Emmanuel Mounier, and the contributors to the review *Esprit* and a Marxist current led by Aragon and directed by the Communist Party.

If the existentialist current, like the last eddies of the surrealist current, carried with it a number of young novelists and helped to create a climate for fictional experiment, the personalist current is entirely dominated by Catholic novelists: Jean Cayrol, Luc Estang (influenced more than any of the others by Bernanos), Paul-André Lesort. In the Marxist current there were, apart from Pierre Coutade, only second-rate novelists, like Elsa Triolet and André Stil, entangled in the rules of 'socialist realism'. Most of the new novelists were exploring their own ways quite outside those traced by philosophers and critics. They turned rather to Balzac, Flaubert and Proust for examples in the practice of their art. They were heirs of a tradition that they admired and it is within the bounds of that tradition that they tried to produce original work.

Marc Bernard

The term novelist is perhaps not quite suitable for the oldest of them, who, like Marc Bernard and Henri Calet, had begun their careers before the war. They were more attracted by veiled confession, the chronicle, the short story or the novella than by the great machinery of the novel.

In *Anny*, 1934, *Pareils à des Enfants*, 1942, then in a series of novels which might be grouped under the title of one of them, *La Belle Humeur*, Marc Bernard shows more interest in the background of the stories he relates – that of adolescence, or of the district around Nîmes from where he comes – than in the stories themselves, or in the characters, who are generally no more than sketches taken from life. A sense of the picturesque, and a certain good-naturedness are the dominant qualities of his tender and piquant tales.

Henri Calet

The work of Henri Calet, who died in 1955, moves by a sort of calm despair disguised by humour. Before the war he travelled a great deal and published works like *La Belle Lurette*, 1935, *Le Mérinos*, 1937 and *Fièvre des Polders*, 1940. Then, in 1945, he published *Le Bouquet*, in which he relates, with the grave humour that is so characteristic of him, his experiences as a prisoner of war. After the Liberation, he became a brilliant journalist. In an inimitable style (that has, in fact, been often imitated), he described the moving and picturesque marginalia of the everyday lives of those most affected by the war, the ordinary people. He treats the capital like a great village which he explores district by district, street by street, revealing unexpected aspects of it and its people. His aim was limited to being an inhabitant of the 14th arrondissement, but he cannot be contained within these limits.

As he became affected by the first symptoms of the disease that was to kill him, Henri Calet ceased to be an amusing writer of occasional articles and became the author of very moving novels like *Le Tout sur le Tout*, 1948, and, above all, of *Monsieur Paul*, 1950. He reveals himself in the play of characters in whom he puts a great deal of himself and of his everyday experiences. An uncompleted novel and a few collections of delightful articles were published after his death.

The work of Henri Calet, with its restrained pathos and controlled, though natural and evocative writing, is valuable as a document on a generation that has not succeeded in its undertakings, on a world that is more oddly absurd than horrible and on a contemporary man who has no future. His is a language of bright, but subtle images. His observations are bold, but utterly lacking in exhibitionism.

Alexandre Vialatte

Alexandre Vialatte first made his name more by his remarkable translations of Kafka than by his novels. His first work, *Battling le Ténébreux*, was published before the war; during the occupation he published *Le Berger Fidèle*, then, in 1951, *Les Fruits du Congo*, one of his best novels.

It is the story of a group of provincial adolescents in a town in the Auvergne and their amorous, sometimes more or less imaginary adventures. They are obsessed with voyages, adventures beyond the seas, impossible love affairs. They are enchanted by a poster, entitled '*Les Fruits du Congo*', which depicts a splendid negress carrying golden-coloured lemons. Their imaginations are fired by the ideas suggested by this poster. The life of the small town in which they are imprisoned is poetically transformed by it: adventures, in which stolid or eccentric bourgeois become implicated, proliferate.

The gang has its own life and atmosphere, which it has itself created. Everything, down to the ordinary details of everyday life, takes on a kind of mad, or at least unexpected and surprising rhythm. The author describes adolescence – eternal adolescence – by its dreams, extravagances and aspirations.

Alexandre Vialatte allows his imagination and sense of fantasy to play upon themes which are of the present but whose drabness become marvellously transformed. He is one of the most accomplished writers of today.

Jean-Louis Curtis

Jean-Louis Curtis, one of the first young novelists to appear after the war, enjoyed a well merited success with *Les Jeunes Hommes*, which relates the moral and spiritual odyssey of young provincials in revolt against their milieu, and with *Les Forêts de la Nuit*, 1947.

He showed himself to possess a precocious mastery of technique. He is not perhaps entirely original, either in his technique (which derives from Aldous Huxley) or in his writing (which remains classical), but he reveals an intelligence of a satirical bent in its observation of manners, and a rare insight into the private motivations of his characters, particularly of adolescents. His portraits of a provincial bourgeoisie which finds its aspirations satisfied by the Vichy régime and his powerful yet subtle picture of the Resistance and the Liberation are astonishingly accurate.

After *Gibier de Potence*, 1949, *Chers Corbeaux*, 1951, which describes often rather savagely the milieu of Saint-Germain-des-Prés, includes a new evocation of the provinces and of the plight of being uprooted from the old life. Curtis rediscovers a fresco-like form in *Les Justes Causes*, 1954, which takes place in the same post-war period as *Les Mandarins*. Some of the best-known figures in the political, literary and artistic worlds are depicted here, under assumed names. Their vanity and ambition are described with humour and cruelty, but at no point do they become mere puppets in the author's hands. It is an excellent piece of documentation on the aspirations and manners of the post-war period.

The work of Jean-Louis Curtis is of its time and concerned with its own peculiar problems. Apart from *Parade* and *Cygne Sauvage*, 1963, he has attempted a few *intimiste* experiments, like *L'Echelle de Soie*, which have not proved very productive. He is a writer who is equally remarkable for his intelligence, his depth of insight and his mastery of writing.

Pierre Gascar

The first novels of Pierre Gascar, *Les Meubles* and *Le Visage Clos,* published before 1950, were influenced by Kafka. The writing is personal, the construction assured. In *Les Bêtes*, 1953, the vision becomes original. By making us enter into the blind world of animals at the mercy of men, Gascar shows, by implication, the cruelty of a humanity without respect for life, without pity for weakness. The cutting up of a calf by a butcher, the flight of horses during an air-raid, the obscure attachments of dogs and cats become so many tragedies in which man is presented as a sorry figure and rises to a vision of a world which never ceases to kill in order to live.

Le Temps des Morts, 1953, combines a poetic vision and a sometimes crude realism. It concerns the experiences of a prisoner of war, but it is not just another piece of documentation. Facts and events contribute to the total vision which is a reflection of the living on the dead. The atrocious condition of the prisoner is softened into a kind of nightmare in a twilight world, at the frontiers of the visible and the invisible.

The subject of *La Graine*, 1955, is childhood, the author's, and of *L'Herbe des Rues*, 1956, adolescence. One is moved by the sobriety of the description and by the touching aspects of 'apprenticeships' that are poor in pleasure and desire. The writing matches the slightest nuances of a stifled sensibility. There are no bravura passages. To depict this greyness of subject the author cleverly distils a poetry of humility.

With *Les Femmes*, then *Soleils*, 1960, in which experiences of love are transformed into so many revelations, Pierre Gascar returns to the short story form of which he is a past master. Thanks to a style that is evocative and rich in implication, he manages to succeed in novels, in which form he feels less at home. *Le Fugitif*, 1961, recreates the melodramatic and romantic atmosphere of a Germany nearing defeat, and *Les Moutons de Feu*, 1963, is inspired by political events nearer to our own time.

It is difficult to decide which of the mass of novelists, of all tendencies, of such diverse inspiration and varied techniques, should be mentioned here in this brief summary. So many have made an appearance only to disappear almost without trace. Some have shown a promise that has remained unfulfilled. Others have persevered, without much success. The stocks rise and fall according to the success of each work. The choice is difficult and personal. It would be misleading to attempt to group all these writers by affinity of attitude, temperament or aim.

In the order in which they appeared after the war one could mention Jean-Louis Bory, with *Mon Village à l'Heure Allemande*, *Le Panier d'Œufs* and more recently *L'Odeur de l'Herbe* – all novels in which fact, characters and sometimes actual events are juxtaposed with vivacity and intelligence.

Paul Gadenne, who died young, had already established himself with two highly personal works, *L'Avenue* and *La Plage de Schveningen.*

Claude Roy revealed himself as an intelligent, brilliant and moving writer of stories inspired by the war and its consequences, as in *La Nuit est le Manteau des Pauvres*, by a humanistic ideology, as in *Le Soleil sur la Terre*, or by his own personal problems, as in *Le Malheur d'Aimer*, 1958.

Jean Bloch-Michel, with *Le Témoin, Les Grandes Circonstances, La Fuite en Egypte, Un Homme Estimable*, reveals himself as a master of the analytical short story in the manner of Benjamin Constant. He is also a moralist who has been influenced by Albert Camus.

Dominique Rolin, who emerged during the war with *Les Marais* remained faithful to a poetic, rather nordic, or Germanic treatment in *Les Deux Soeurs,* 1946, and *Le Souffle,* 1952, before writing the frank, almost raw *Moi qui ne suis qu'un Amour*, 1958, *Le Lit*, 1960, and coming under the influence of the 'new novel'.

Beatrix Beck has an ability to transform the most insignificant incidents in her life into taut, well-articulated, moving stories: *Barny,* 1948, *Une Mort Irrégulière*, 1951, above all *Léon Morin, Prêtre*, 1952, and, more recently, *Le Muet*, 1963.

Célia Bertin made a notable début with *Parade des Impies*, 1946, and was awarded the Prix Renaudot in 1953 for *La Dernière Innocence*. She has recently published *La Comédienne*, 1963.

Marguerite Yourcenar, who before the war had published a number of analytical stories, discovered her true path and had considerable success with *Les Mémoires d'Hadrien*, which helped to bring the historical novel back into fashion.

Claire Sainte-Soline showed assured gifts as a novelist and consummate technique in a number of works of which the most remarkable was perhaps *Le Dimanche des Rameaux*, 1952.

Françoise Mallet-Joris, who enjoyed a certain *succès de scandale* with a story full of acute observation and somewhat cynical frankness, *Le Rempart des Béguines*, 1951, acquired deeper qualities that became apparent in long, rather Balzacian novels like *Les Mensonges*, 1956, and *L'Empire Céleste*, 1958, before embarking on other *genres*, such as the historical novel and the day-to-day journal, which have made her more than a feminine novelist.

Quite the opposite in inspiration and manner is Marcel Schneider, who is more poet than novelist. In *Le Granit et l'Absence*, 1947, *Cueillir le Romarin*, 1948, *Le Chasseur Vert*, 1950, and other novels in which he creates with a strange, delicate fantasy that springs directly from the German romantics a world of mysterious occultists and magic journeys.

Raymond Abellio, who does not possess the stylistic qualities of Marcel Schneider, has gone further in the interpretation of Tradition, of which he is a convinced adept to the point of didacticism. He finds in it new sources of romanticism, new perspectives from which to view contemporary events, which in turn take on an unusual appearance, as in *Heureux les Pacifiques*, 1947, *Les Yeux d'Ezéchiel sont ouverts*, 1952, and above all in *La Fosse de Babel*, 1962, a mystical summa of our times which is animated with genuine inspiration.

In a more classical *genre*, a mixture of traditional realism and analysis, mention must be made, because of his exceptional talent, of José Cabanis, a painter of provincial souls, who draws with a few sharp lines, rather in the manner of Jouhandeau, as in *L'Auberge Fameuse*, 1953, and *Juliette Bonviolle*, 1954. In *Le Fils*, 1956, *Le Bonheur du Jour*, 1961, and *Les Cartes du Temps*, 1962, with which he has gradually emerged as a novelist of the first rank, he has explored a rich autobiographical background.

In *La Prison Maritime*, 1961, Michel Mohrt has attempted to renovate the traditional novel by returning to its origins in the past.

Also autobiographical was *La Gana*, 1958, by Jean Douassot, which caused a sensation with its crude realism – a realism, however, which is not over-emphatic and is transmuted by a poetry of places, characters and circumstances which raises it to a mysterious surreality, such as is experienced by a child who transforms into fantasy the sordid world in which he lives. Jean Douassot creates a region that is situated half-way between dream and reality. He uses great washes of lyricism which in no way blind him to what is happening around him. With highly personal humour, he exaggerates reality to the point of caricature, as in *Sens Inverses*, 1960. He is possessed of a natural strength that is reminiscent of Henry Miller, and guided by an infallible instinct which some critics have even described as a gift of 'clairvoyance'. Douassot accumulates his discoveries along his own lonely path.

There is the unusual talent of Boris Vian, a despairing humorist in *L'Ecume des Jours, L'Automne à Pékin*, 1956, and a number of posthumous collections. Ladislas Dormandi is a punctilious realist in *L'Autre Rive* and an eccentric in other novels.

The talent of Geneviève Serreau is bitter, poetic, passionately devoted to the discovery of truth. Her *Le Soldat Bourquin,* 1955, and *Le Fondateur*, 1959, cover the great movements in sensibility of the times. In *Ressac*, 1962, under the combined influences of Faulkner and Beckett, but using a quite personal technique, she attains a sort of enigmatic perfection which makes her one of the most likeable novelists writing today.

What was called before and during the Algerian War the 'North African School' comprises a number of quite different young novelists of differing qualities: Mouloud Feraoun, Mohammed Dib, Mouloud Mammeri, Albert Memmi (*La Statue de Sel*), and above all Kateb Yacine who, in *Nedjma*, 1956, relates a horrifying story (the colonialist extortions in Algeria) to the ancestral myths of his country. Many of them were first encouraged to write by their generous and colourful compatriot of European origin, the novelist Emmanuel Roblès.

This very incomplete review which excludes (apart from those who may have been forgotten) many successful or well-known novelists, who have been content to exploit, or even to perfect, a malleable fictional formula, which is suitable to any message and can serve any purpose, provides none the less an impression of the richness and variety of the material. It is a wide range indeed, that stretches from the 'natural' writer to the most scrupulous stylist, from the competent craftsman to the great artist. It is tone, manner and qualities of writing that are the distinguishing features of the novelist, not the different *genres* of novel he writes, whether realistic, poetic, psychological or fantastic. Each explores his own chosen country, makes discoveries that can be important or merely incidental, and each attains a greater or less degree of success. They are all seeking a personal voice that will be recognisable among others. And if posterity deals its blows, even among those we have mentioned, they will none the less have acted as audible witnesses of their times and proved worthy of the confidence of a period often only too chaotic and of a post-war humanity a little unsteady on its feet. Between 'commitment' and the ivory tower, the field of expression is wide enough for those who wish to use words in a way that is not entirely vulgar.

11 *The Novel in Question*

In publishing *Qu'est-ce que la Littérature?*, in which he attempted to define a phenomenology of literary creation, Jean-Paul Sartre was not opening up virgin territory. Already, before the war, certain surrealists admitted that they had turned to literature 'out of weakness'. Some of their followers may have expressed, even excessively, their confidence in literature; others who had felt more or less deeply the same influence, did not devote themselves to literature with an easy conscience. The process of literature remained open. It had gone as far as to question language itself.

Georges Bataille

Twenty years after it was written, Georges Bataille published a novel, *Le Bleu du Ciel*, 1957. He is also the author of erotic stories, published either in semi-secrecy (*Histoire de l'Oeil, Madame Edwarda*) or quite openly, like *L'Abbé*, 1950. Outside all *genres* and categories, unconcerned about sacrificing anything to the novel or to what is generally called 'poetry', the author of *L'Expérience Intérieure*, 1943, *Le Coupable*, 1943, *Haine de la Poésie*, 1946, has invented a *genre* which combines stark confession, philosophical reflection and mystical search. He obeys no rules, other than that of making himself understood, and he contravenes all prohibitions, social or moral. Engaged in a quest of the absolute, he proceeds in every direction that is opened to him. He wishes to consider literature as above all a means of expression and language as an instrument. He uses them to communicate experiences which are, in any case, outside them.

Georges Bataille is possessed by what he calls 'the will to the impossible'. He would like to consider his experiment as useless, with no other end than *le néant*, nothingness, from which it emerges. He cannot, however, extract himself from this experiment. So how does one assume this contradiction? By a number of kinds of behaviour: laughter, games, ecstasy (erotic or mystical), meditation (as understood in *yoga* or *zen*), poetic expression. All are capable of leading us into the realm of 'sovereignty', of universal communication.

Given this aim, the novel is no more than a pitiful means. Even poetry is often no more than an 'evocation'; it jumbles the order of words, without changing the order of things. Why does one write? In order to become aware of the very movement by which all experience, of whatever kind, leads into nothingness. Writing is a residue. Thoughts, desires, dreams and obsessions may be its material, but Bataille refuses to exploit that material. It should be no more than the tracks of a movement towards the unknown. It marks the effects of a struggle that takes place elsewhere and which it is in nobody's power to stop. It is the struggle that was waged by Pascal, Sade, Rimbaud, Nietzsche. They threw themselves into it in all innocence. Bataille knows that success will bring with it his own defeat. He accepts this, and does so with gaiety, knowing that literature is an allurement, and that this allurement is the most precious evidence of what man aspires to.

Maurice Blanchot

For Maurice Blanchot, who pursues a parallel activity as critic (his work in this field is both original and important) and as novelist, the nothingness, which is at the limit of Bataille's experiences, is to be found in the nature of language itself.

He does not believe that the writer 'wants to say something' or to use his gifts to create an equivalent of the world. If he does in fact do this, it occurs at the end of a movement by which the world has first been revealed as an absence, and the 'word' as a privileged mode of silence. The writer has, in fact, 'nothing to say'. At the same time, 'he must say this nothing'. It is his function to do so, his *raison d'être*. The words translate an original silence and leads whoever proffers them to the essential silence. All literature is based upon this movement. It is as if, from a certain moment onwards, the word was not the work of the writer. It is a reality which is outside and beyond things, which exists independently of the writer; it possesses its own laws, and often passes unrecognized. Kafka wished to write like Flaubert, Baudelaire envied Théophile Gautier. It is as if they had been condemned to writing 'like' Kafka or 'like' Baudelaire. Maurice Blanchot goes as far as believing that literature is above all the domain of the 'as if'.

Language denies what it names: 'In order to say "this woman", I must in some way or other extract her from her reality of flesh and bones, render her absent, annihilate her. The word gives me the being, but it gives me it deprived of being. It is the absence of this being, its nothingness, what remains of it when it has lost being, that is, the simple fact that it is not.' Language is negation and destruction. That is its first movement. But it also exists, and by its existence alone, it affirms. That is its second movement. The third to which it attains and which is its end, unites this affirmation that denies (existence) and this negation that affirms (being); it carries death into life and life into death. 'Death', he writes, 'is man's possibility, it is his chance; it is by death that the future of a finished world is left to us; death is man's great hope, his only hope.'

In *Thomas l'Obscur, Aminadab, Le Très-Haut*, published during and after the war, Blanchot incarnates these metaphysical views that were the result of reflection on the nature of language. These novels, which remind one at first of Kafka, are not immediately 'readable'. Their power is rather one of magic and fascination, which is created by the very virtues of a writing which seems to efface reality as it evokes it. Everything takes place in a half light in which events exist like will-o'-the-wisps, disappearing even more quickly than they appear, and in which characters are only half seen. These works are not really 'novels' at all, but narrations, each stage of which is a step in a solitary quest that is personal to the author. There is no certainty that from work to work the quest makes any progress. It is ceaselessly recommenced as the end ceaselessly retreats.

Certain more recent works – *L'Arrêt de Mort, Au Moment*

Voulu, Celui qui ne m'accompagnait pas, Le Dernier Homme, L'Attente, L'Oubli, exhibit a perfect rigour of writing and an admirable sense of movement, but one utterly obscure as far as the author's intentions are concerned. The reader can sense an atmosphere of absence, or of non-presence, which expresses the essential void that lies at the heart of the world and at the heart of man. Language, which is called upon to fill this void, appears as pure discourse, a clever play of words, an expression of the inexpressible, as insubstantial. Though devoid of references to what we usually call reality, the work of Maurice Blanchot gives the impression of apprehending an essential reality that cannot be expressed.

Louis-René des Forêts

Louis-René des Forêts is haunted by the same problems: that of making language adequate to experience and that of the ultimate aims of literature in general and of the novel in particular. After a rather Faulknerian novel, *Les Mendiants*, which was published in 1943, Louis-René des Forêts was content to write fewer and fewer short stories and novellas, such as *Le Bavard*, 1946, and *La Chambre des Enfants*, 1960.

Le Bavard is in fact the story of a quiet man who, one evening, in extraordinary circumstances, starts talking a very great deal. There follows a series of catastrophes and a feeling of shame from which he does not seem able to absolve himself. He revokes the main lines of his narrative: is he not in fact beginning once more to talk too much, that is to lie and show conceit? Literature is this 'talking too much'. Its only excuse lies in its possibility of leading to silence.

La Chambre des Enfants is a collection of five strongly linked stories of which the heroes are either mutes or individuals who exercise silence, as a game or as a discipline, or peculiarly laconic people. There is also a singer, that is, someone who uses speech in a very special way. The author shows that silence can be a form of nobility, or a very effective form of revolt. To speak is to participate in the inanity of universal noise. It is also, paradoxically, to give to speech an importance that it can never fulfil in the world of everyday relations. In the case of the singer, it becomes the expression, on the plane of art, of the best that the individual has in him.

It is in this ambivalent movement of valorization, sometimes from silence, sometimes from words, that the works of Louis-René des Forêts develop. He takes a bitter pleasure in parodying his own procedure, in criticizing the very basis of the work he has undertaken. If there is no writer less innocent than he, there are few who attain such mastery of their instrument. Again, it is the personal quest of the author that is uppermost. Nevertheless, he provides us with enough matter – dreams, hauntings, obsessions – to allow us to participate in his work and communicate with him.

The trial to which language is submitted, the refusal to petrify discourse in fixed forms, in short, the questioning of literature by itself constitutes the constant interrogation of a means of expression which, like all art, tries by doing so to renew its forms and techniques. Whereas in the other arts, this questioning results in spectacular revolutions (which lead sometimes to new fashions and new dogmas), the art of words, the art of narration, has much greater difficulties to overcome. It is easy to claim that one does not 'understand' an abstract painting or a piece of dodecaphonic music, but one cannot give up trying to understand a novel. Literary discourse is communication *par excellence*. To throw doubt upon its possibility is to doubt the possibility of communication altogether. But the modern novel has entered this narrow passage, in which it constantly suffers the risk of being crushed. It has carried its investigations to the point at which it has discovered something new.

12 *The Neo-Classical Reaction*

In about 1950 a change of climate occurred with the appearance of writers who, for the most part, had not taken part in the events of 1940, though they had been affected by their consequence. They were ill at ease in post-Liberation France.

While not exactly losing influence, Sartre was no longer capable of arousing the same interest as before. In abusing despair, the absurd and violence, the existentialist novel revealed its excesses and its weaknesses. This eclipse of existentialism on the philosophical and literary planes coincided with the end of the illusions that inspired the Resistance and with a return to the pre-war *status quo*. With the feeling that fundamentally 'nothing has changed' or that 'everything has returned to what it was before', commitment revealed its ineffectualness. Those who only a few years previously had given so much of themselves had now condemned themselves, or seen themselves condemned to introspection; and from this development sprang an increasingly obvious lack of interest in public affairs. 'Since we cannot do anything any more, let us confine ourselves to exercising our profession' – such appeared to be the rather over-simplified but perhaps justified reasoning of many writers.

The newcomers of the 1950s settled into this attitude of mind and contributed to its spread. Post-war disillusion turned into accusations against those who strove to renew the moral, spiritual and intellectual state of the nation. In any case, said the newcomers, it was a task that did not concern the writer. Let us return to fine language, well-made novels, gratuitousness, relaxation and escape. In place of the novel with a message and metaphysical ambitions, they wished to substitute a novel that was amusing, witty, 'well-written'. The only commandment which the review *La Parisienne* wished to obey was 'thou shalt please'. An end to the desire to shock, to crude brutality, to jargon! The masters claimed by Jacques Laurent, Roger Nimier and Antoine Blondin were men who in varying degrees had been collaborators or who at least had not been members of the Resistance: Jacques Chardonne, a fine and sensitive stylist, Paul Morand, a fashionable novelist of the twenties, the humorist Marcel Aymé, who, in a rather ambiguous essay preached 'intellectual comfort', Jean Giono, who had escaped from the upheavals of the century into the past, a Stendhal reduced to the size of a *petit maître*. This return to a recent or distant past was accompanied by a more or less overt contempt for new forms and techniques and for a renewal of language, and, at best, by a desire for a classicism of clarity and formal perfection. To these one might usually add a cast of mind that would like to be thought of as elegant, irreverent and even at times insolent. They wished to break with 'didactic' writing and the 'black novel'. They made fun of whatever was 'serious'.

Jacques Laurent

Jacques Laurent, who, under the name of Cécil Saint-Laurent, wrote lengthy, highly successful popular novels, such as *Caroline Chérie*, assumed the leadership of the adversaries of Jean-Paul Sartre and literature 'with a message'. In a number of clever, often brilliant, articles, he attacked existentialism and its disciples, depicting them as stupid, boring and heavy, in the manner of 'German philosophers'. He attempts to bring humour to his side by comparing Sartre with Paul Bourget, another didactic novelist.

A prolific writer, who has tried his hand at most kinds of writing, Jacques Laurent has also succeeded in writing novels, such as *Les Corps Tranquilles* and *Le Petit Canard*, that lack neither talent nor insight.

Roger Nimier

In spite of his sometimes blatant frivolity, Roger Nimier seems to take his literary vocation more seriously than Jacques Laurent.

He began with a good novel, *Les Epées*, which, despite provocations of all kinds (the work begins with a scene of masturbation), reveals a born novelist. The case of its hero, who passes through boredom, insolence and also perhaps through despair, from the Resistance to the Army, is probably similar to that of other upper-class young men who have sought blindly among events for reasons for doing something, rather than really acting. In his best book, *Le Hussard Bleu*, 1950, in which he depicts a French regiment during the occupation of a district of defeated Germany, Nimier seems to be influenced both by Stendhal and Céline. He employs brilliantly, though without much conviction, all the fashionable techniques from the interior monologue to slang dialogue. His heroes are avowed cynics, often blest with a true Parisian wit: while pointing irreverent fun at everything, including themselves, the 'hussards' are careful not to overstep the bounds of permitted insolence. They are certainly not rebels: they are little more than licensed jesters. Their own vacuity frightens them. It is the vacuity of a generation that believes in nothing.

After this brilliant beginning, Roger Nimier suffered a marked decline in power with his *Les Enfants Tristes*, 1951 – the children of the title are really no more than spoilt – and *Histoire d'un Amour*, 1953, a linear exercise devoid of any warmth or even of life. No more was heard of him until he was killed at an early age in a car crash.

Although he was a good writer, Roger Nimier lacked the qualities that might have made him an important one – the ability to enlarge his horizon and understand a boredom which was the result of adolescence and of the time in which he lived, and of which he might have extracted something quite different. Frivolity is not always a mask for shyness. But it prevented him from becoming a witness to whom we might have gone for a knowledge of a generation who wished above all to be 'uncommitted'.

Antoine Blondin

The author of *L'Europe Buissonière*, 1949, *Les Enfants du Bon Dieu*, 1952, *L'Humeur Vagabonde*, 1955, strove not only to please, but to charm. He succeeded effortlessly in these novels intentionally set outside time and divorced from the contemporary world, whose characters would have criticized as a lack of tact the slightest display of seriousness. They pass from adventure to adventure, never settling in any one place, like spring butterflies, meeting events without any desire to know them, taking care when they touch each other not to damage their delicate wings. Their heads are not as light as one might think and they are sometimes visited by vague anxieties, but they refuse to treat them tragically. In the game of life, the pleasant things outweigh the unpleasant too much not to take the latter with humour or to allow themselves to be caught up in the cogs of the social machine. Flee from responsibilities of all kinds (even those created by love), do not ask questions one is not capable of answering, emerge unscathed from every encounter – such seem to be the principles of Antoine Blondin's philosophy.

This charming but somewhat summary philosophy was particularly marked in *Un Singe en Hiver*, 1959, in which the author revealed something of his personal drama. It could now be seen that the charm was perhaps a disguise for loneliness. Like Roger Nimier before him, Antoine Blondin is, without admitting it, looking for a little human warmth, a semblance of fraternity.

Bernard Pingaud

Jacques Laurent, Roger Nimier and Antoine Blondin are avowed 'reactionaries', in literature as in politics. The case of Bernard Pingaud is more complex. He too reacted against the current fashions, expressing himself in a classical language which eschewed all 'effects' and strove after a cold, glazed quality. But gradually he became more receptive to the problems of the times, to the point of renouncing his first loves. It is a long way from *Mon Beau Navire*, his first novel, and even from *L'Amour Triste,* 1950, which narrowly missed the Prix Goncourt, to *Prisonnier*, 1958, in which a philosophical influence (a void is at the heart of Being as at the centre of love) and a search for a new novel form are highly marked. The author is more intelligent than sensitive, more a critic than someone possessed by the demons of creation. It is obvious that behind his heroes is himself: fragile, hurt, anxious, trying to defend himself against this anxiety by a play of dialectic, which, resting on the slight ledge of Being, opens on to nothingness. It is a situation he states with honesty and lucidity.

Françoise Sagan

Françoise Sagan also belongs to that generation of young novelists who tried to express what separated them from preceding generations. In spite of an unexpected and extraordinary success that is difficult to account for, she is not the most gifted of them. But if she is classed among women novelists, her originality becomes apparent at once. Although she too is preoccupied with writing about love, she speaks of it neither with the sentimentality, nor the occasional aggressiveness one is accustomed to meeting in female novelists. And the lucidity, the serene despair, the detachment with which she describes love affairs that could be highly moving is even more striking than her amoral naturalism. A girl is jealous of her father's mistress: she manages to arrange her death. This is the entire subject of *Bonjour Tristesse*. The same girl falls in love with a man in his forties, only to find the same boredom she had hoped to escape by loving him: *Un Certain Sourire*. They are simple stories, unelaborate and written in a classical, highly restrained style. Yet the restraint of manner conceals great audacity of purpose. These delicate stories describe the quiet, silent emancipation of a generation that has ratified the failure of its elders and which is no longer concerned with the rules of 'good breeding' and goes its own way. She wishes to live according to her own rules. She has no illusions.

Dans un Mois dans un An reveals a more ambitious subject, but the qualities that have gone to make Françoise Sagan's success are minor ones, though they are exploited with talent. She exhibits them brilliantly in each new work, but she has not as yet either deepened or renewed them.

13 *Beyond the Novel*

The reputation of the young novelists of 1950 was not to last long. Jacques Laurent did not write another work that measured up to the disturbance he had caused. Roger Nimier turned to journalism and publishing. Despite his efforts at renewal, Antoine Blondin became the prisoner of his own legend. After a brief period of entrenchment, the movement which brought writers to create new novel-forms, to express as clearly as possible that indecipherable reality of which literature is made, began once more. First, with the resurrection of the *Nouvelle Revue Française,* which, against the exaggerations of some, and the nostalgia of others, advertised its single-minded concern for literary quality before everything else; then, with *Lettres Nouvelles*, a revue which was more attracted to novelty and which claimed to represent a 'changing literature'. Above all, new novelists like Jean Reverzy and such writers as Pierre Klossowski and Samuel Beckett pursued what became the investigation of reality through language, whether this investigation took the form of the novel or not.

Jean Reverzy

A doctor who had turned to literature relatively late, Jean Reverzy made a sensational beginning with *Le Passage*, 1954. It tells the story of a man dying – a man suffering from an incurable disease, who, after a lifetime spent in Tahiti where he had first gone out of wanderlust, returns to his native town to die. He is helped by a doctor who enables him to die a less painful death. They are both moved by the same calm despair. The truth of life is loneliness and death. Everything else is useless noise, vanity.

The work is not remarkable for any particular innovation.

Composed like a poem in which recur certain leitmotive, it provides so obvious a vision of our condition that the work itself seems to represent an answer to man's anguish.

The great subject (and the major obsession) of the author is death. This is even more apparent in *Place des Angoisses*. With material drawn from autobiographical memories, Reverzy shows the commanding role that death plays in the battlefield in which human beings struggle hopelessly to live. It is a law to which we are all subject, with decrees that admit no appeal, and to which succumb even those who are charged with the task of softening the blows, the doctors.

After these two novels, Jean Reverzy, forcibly struck by both the capabilities and the limitations of this instrument, writing, which he had so far used above all to free himself of an obsession, decided to use it in creation *ex nihilo*. In *Le Corridor*, 1957, he sets up dummies which he wishes to bring to life by virtue of language alone. He wishes to verify in what way the particular language of the writer differs from ordinary language, which he compares to a *flatus vocis*, by what mystery it can give birth to life, while ordinary language serves merely to disguise the slow decline of man towards death. He even postulates 'a new science which will be concerned with the approach of human beings, their contact, their retreat, and the movements of their bodies and limbs', in short, everything that language is particularly powerless to express, and yet at the same time supposed to express. Moreover, he condemns his previous works, which he considers to be too 'literary'. Obsessed as he is by death, he wishes to capture life at its source, to show what essentially it consists of. He succeeds in doing so in an exercise which does not conceal the standpoint from which it was written. The conclusion arrived at came no doubt as a surprise to the author himself; that life thus manifested is almost indistinguishable from dream and nightmare. The realism of the detailed descriptions, which are intended to be no more than descriptive, is none the less transcended by vision. It reminds one of Kafka.

Le Corridor is no more than the first stage in a development that was to lead the writer to the discovery of unknown territory.

Unfortunately, he died – he had an intuition of his early death and expected it – before being able to reach it. In his posthumous works, *Le Silence de Cambridge, La Vraie Vie*, 1960, he showed himself to be still preoccupied with language, but anxious to note the new themes that nourished his obsession. He disappeared before completing the great life-work he had undertaken.

Pierre Klossowski

A theologian and commentator on the works of Sade, a Catholic who cultivates heresy and a mystic of eroticism, a notable essayist and a distinguished translator, Pierre Klossowski, who was a close friend of Rilke and of Gide, came to the novel almost by chance. He began with a short theological story, *La Vocation Suspendue*, 1950, in which he illustrated two tendencies struggling at the heart of the Church, the 'devotional' and the 'inquisitional', then went on to write a triptych: *Roberte ce Soir*, 1950, *La Révocation de l'Edit de Nantes*, 1959, and *Le Souffleur*, 1960. These works are, in appearance at least, theological stories in which purely theoretical discussions about the relations of the soul and the body, or of spiritual salvation, are given free rein. They are of interest only to specialists. On the other hand, the situations which give rise to these discussions and in which they are embodied are in themselves truly fictional.

In *Roberte ce Soir*, in which the heroine practises to the limit the rules of hospitality, that is, offers herself willingly and before her husband's eyes to any guest who happens to show a desire for her, the entire problem is whether she should consent to give herself to her nephew who lives under the same roof as herself. True, she is not only a body of which the first comer may avail himself, but if, from a theological point of view the body is nothing, is no more than the envelope of the soul, every expression of this body is permissible, and even becomes a condition of spiritual progress. The argument is specious. It allows the writer to push an audacious discovery into regions in which, outside any moral consideration, eroticism becomes a category of the human being, not a means of pleasure, but a door opening on to knowledge.

In *La Révocation de l'Edit de Nantes*, the scholastic aspect of Klossowski's work is effaced in the interests of a more complex story composed of situations that throw strange light on human behaviour. Roberte is no longer *woman*, but a woman, socially and even politically situated (she is a Radical deputy and a member of the legislative commission for censorship), who is no longer satisfied by marital legitimacy. She discovers the world of sexual perversion and imposes on herself the duty of exploring it without either emotion or remorse, in perfect equanimity of soul. It is the very condition of her quest that it sometimes appears farcical, sometimes scandalous. She believes that until scandal becomes quite normal to her she will not be completely free. She becomes so only by shaking off the yoke of her husband, an old theologian, who, although he pushes the arguments for acceptance to the limit, fails to accept behaviour that is at once aberrant and 'natural'.

The work contains allusions and implications which only a philosopher could unravel. The layman is content to be moved, sometimes profoundly so, by a poetic atmosphere of religious and erotic mystery which sets one's nerves tingling. There is no question on the part of the author of deliberate provocation, and if he chooses to describe unsavoury situations, it is with an unquestionable seriousness of purpose. He expresses, in a way that is perhaps not altogether coherent, a mythology that we have seen flourish elsewhere: apart from the personal preoccupations of the author, it is to be found in a certain current of demoniacal surrealism (this is even more apparent in *Le Souffleur*, which is situated at the limit of the 'black novel'), in the discoveries of Georges Bataille and in the fictional creations of Maurice Blanchot. Here too, the writer is trying by means of language to conquer a certain unknown, which, once discovered, would make man and the world comprehensible. The resistances which prevent him from succeeding reside in the nature of himself. Pierre Klossowski seems to be trying to break down these resistances consciously and methodically. Man is more than man, he implies everything he has thought and believed for thousands of years: the language which is himself and yet which does not belong to him. The enterprise of destruction is endless. Supposing that one day the work will be completed, would we then discover among the rubble Being, the Absolute? Pierre Klossowski, having posited this absolute at the beginning of his quest, was later to see it as a dead end.

Samuel Beckett

Samuel Beckett is Irish and published his early works in English. But he wrote most of his novels and plays, in French. Today he is among the greatest of 'French' writers, and some people consider him the most important.

The first novel published in French, *Murphy*, 1947, passed almost unnoticed. It tells the story of an anxious man who finds satisfaction in a job as a male nurse in a lunatic asylum, then, feeling unsatisfied after all, kills himself. *Molloy*, 1951, is also the story of a quest: Molloy sets off to visit his dying mother, gets lost in the town, then in the country, then in a forest in which he crawls forward on hands and knees, before falling unconscious into a ditch. Moran, his father, sets out in turn in search of his son and returns home months later without having found him. In *Malone Meurt*, 1951, a dying man, to pass the time and escape boredom, tells stories that are generally without significance and that he mixes up with each other. In *L'Innommable*, 1953, the narrator becomes confused with the author, who accuses himself of talking in order to obscure his own story, the only one which was worth telling, and which he is unable to tell. In the end, he is no more than 'a big, stupid, red, thick-lipped, slobbery mouth, tirelessly emptying itself, with the noise of washing and big kisses, of the words that obstruct it'. In *Comment c'est*, 1961, man is reduced to a state of larva and merges into the mud in which he is crawling about. The world means no more to him than a meaningless confusion of noises. His own language consists only of unconnected words, onomatopoeias and rumblings.

These narratives trace a movement: from words to silence,

from life (even a precarious one) to death (in life). As they develop, Beckett's 'heroes' become more and more deprived of their physical capacities, more and more withdrawn from the bustle of the world, take refuge more and more in their own minds, losing the use of memory and of their senses, reduced to a pure consciousness that comes to possess, exclusively, but with infinite power, the capacity to suffer. Murphy progresses in everyday reality and kills himself by a deliberate act. With *Molloy*, the everyday world is distorted and draws us into a waking dream in which the characters suffer a noticeable depreciation on all levels. The case of Malone is worse, since he is going to die; old and paralysed, he is already close to the condition of an animal. The speaker in *L'Innommable* has no identity and no memory and is incapable of forming coherent thoughts. He wonders if he is anything more than the form of the words he pronounces. Beyond life and death, he must complete an absurd task: that of speaking. The two characters of *Comment c'est* become indistinguishable from the mud in which they are engulfed. We have thus passed from normal humanity to inhumanity through all the degradations possible in a human being. At the end of this quest, there is nothing left but Nothingness. We are bubbles that burst one after another on the surface of a miry pond, with a soft noise that we call existence.

'Nothing is more real than nothing', Beckett affirms. Yet nothing is not a form of absolute more easy to attain than others, and literature would come to deny what a consciousness affirms, if it really was a question here of literature, consciousness and affirmation, of references to an order and to values. Beckett's questioning of everything is itself under question: it is the description of a state of fact, not a protest. The anger, often humorous and joyful, of the human being in fetters, satisfies itself and consumes itself with a kind of terrible alacrity; it requires no other stimulus and even makes us doubt whether it really is anger. It could after all be nothing more than a faithful account of the progressive decomposition of the world and of man, of a disaster, tending towards a nothingness that is never attained (that would be peace at last) and that we have not yet perceived. Anger being no more than 'words', the 'care for the truth' would direct the words, breaking over them like a command.

A questioning of the world and of man? The first gradually loses its appearances to the point at which it is transformed into a cell isolated in space, abstracted from time and bathed eternally in a constant soft light. In it lies an invalid, who is generally deaf, dumb and blind (except when he reduces himself to a single, unmoving perpetually open eye), who soon becomes no more than a being, or the myth of a being, subsisting inside some monstrous envelope. He becomes confused with the author, who destroys his previous constructions by showing (as in *L'Innommable*) what lies they were made out of, and who disappears himself, *qua* speaking subject, to be replaced by an anonymous and uncontrolled voice that produces only meaningless noises. What, then, are these works? Self-indulgence, lies, deception? He was obliged to create, but he is equally obliged to denounce its vanity and hypocrisy. That royal creator, language, is also a destroyer: words are all equally inane. 'Supposing I were to say babababa,' wonders the author, and in considering in a voice no more than the noise it makes he in fact ends up with a sort of 'babababa'. There remains only the reality of the cenesthesic sensations, only suffering.

The questioning of language is accompanied by a questioning of the work. Condemned to speak, Beckett's heroes spend their time denying what they have just affirmed, saying *yes* and *no* at the same time. If one has to speak, then at least let it be about nothing. In the regions in which Beckett moves and in which the work dissolves in a fog of meaninglessness as it is being created, it is easy to believe that nothing is said. And yet no words seem to me to be more essential than his.

The achievement of Samuel Beckett marks the end of a trial of literature, language and speech. It is now impossible to move further towards silence through the word. The author is now left with only one alternative: to stop writing or to repeat himself. His theatrical work, from *En attendant Godot* to *La Dernière Bande* and *Oh les Beaux Jours!* follows a parallel movement. In the end there is only one character on the stage speaking. The ultimate reality remains the word, but a word that is meaningless and whose very inanity is laughable.

It is at ourselves that we are laughing, bitterly. No writer has to this degree given the impression that his voice was ours, that they are indefinitely interchangeable, that we are speaking through his mouth and he for us. Communication has become communion. The work of literature fades before the ultimate realities of life, and finds, in this effacement, its truth.

14 *The 'Nouveau Roman'*

The 'New Novel' is a useful term, first used by journalists, to denote a number of experiments, which, in the anarchy of individual exploration, converged in the refusal of certain novel-forms – the psychological novel or novel of character analysis, the novel of passion or of action – and their replacement by a narrative that was concerned less with the conventions of *genres* than with the particular reality demanding expression. But what reality? From this point opinions diverge. It would be erroneous to believe that because the practitioners of the new novel share the same refusal they are pursuing the same ends. Nathalie Sarraute and Alain Robbe-Grillet have tried to theorize their views, but not only do these views not agree, the results to which they lead are very different. The same differences exist between the work of Michel Butor and that of Claude Simon, Roger Pinget or Claude Ollier. the 'new novel' forms neither a school, nor even a movement.

In a collection of essays called *L'Ere du Soupçon*, Nathalie Sarraute convincingly demonstrates the progressive decline of the traditional components of the novel as imagined by the writers of the nineteenth century. Plot, to the construction of which they lavished all their attention, characters, which they tried to make both 'living' and 'typical', the care they displayed in studying the development of their heroes in a time and a place that were as solid as rock, or in making them 'reveal' themselves on certain special occasions (a personal crisis, a moment of great temptation, the fatality of events or of situations) – it is clear that their great successors at the beginning of the present century paid no heed to all these things. Joyce thought so little of plot that he superimposed the adventures of Bloom on those of the hero of the *Odyssey*; the plots of *The Trial* and *The Castle* are practically non-existent and Kafka's characters are more like a god composed of a number of persons and who, as far as one can see, bears a strange affinity with the author. The word 'message' has been fashionable for so long only because it represented something real: through the medium of his 'story', his characters and the adventures that befell them, the writer was really communicating news about himself. In the end, we came to be interested only in this news. Writers and readers alike have shown less and less interest in the strictly 'fictional' aspect of the novel, and more and more in what the work conceals and what it reveals – the particular mode of man's being in the world. By a natural development, the novel has passed from encyclopaedic description (of the world and of human passions) to the moral, poetic, philosophical or metaphysical appropriation of this world by a privileged individual, the author. It is his personal vision, more than his 'creation' which matters – the original and plausible expression that, through his work, he provides of the world and his relations with it. It is in his work that the writer often reveals himself most completely: Joyce in *Ulysses*, rather than in his disappointing letters, Kafka, less timidly and more coherently in *The Trial* or *The Castle* than in the notes of his journal. At this limit, with subjectivity triumphant, the novel disappears as a *genre* and becomes pure expression.

If Robbe-Grillet is in agreement with Nathalie Sarraute on the correctness of this diagnosis, if he believes that a novel can no longer consist of a plot and characters and that it is necessary to declare 'the death of the character', together with that of the psychological and philosophical categories (time, space) in which the character is imprisoned, he wishes, on the other hand, to break with the process which is taking the novel towards a greater and greater degree of subjectivity. He asks the author to forget himself, or even to eliminate himself, and to show what he has to show. Let us rid the novel of characters: too often they are mere substitutes for the author on to which he projects 'meanings' that are foreign to them. Similarly, instead of showing things as they are, he sees them through the distortion of his own personality. He is conditioned by a historical situation, a particular environment, a particular culture: 'he fails to see the world around him with open eyes'. More frequently, he 'animates' things (that is, he discovers a soul in them), he humanizes them. But the world is presented to us in its pure existence, solid and obstinately itself, impregnable: 'All round us, defying the onslaught of our animistic or domesticating adjectives, things *are there*. Their surface is clear, smooth and *intact*, but without false glamour, without transparency.' For Robbe-Grillet, the novel must be a scrupulously drawn up inventory of what is perceived by our senses, of the world that exists outside us: the pure world of the object, the world of the 'thing-in-itself'. He hopes that this world will communicate its verisimilitude and solidity to the world of the novel.

Perhaps it is a vain hope. It is neither possible nor desirable that the novelist should strive to become a pure conscience-reflection and deploy all his forces to 'desocializing' himself. Moreover, the form of expression used in the novel, writing, is an instrument that is 'personalized' by the novelist himself for certain definite ends. How can the world of objects remain purely gratuitous when it participates in a human and historical world? How can it be abstracted from time and space, or be thought impervious to any charge or transformation? The *littérature du constat* – the literature of statement – announced by Robbe-Grillet's friend, Roland Barthes, would be the literature of an invisible world.

Alain Robbe-Grillet

In his novels Robbe-Grillet has attempted to provide the first examples of this 'objective' literature. The town in *Les Gommes,* with its streets, its houses and its canal, is the dominant 'presence' of the novel. On the other hand, the characters enjoy no more than a shadowy existence, silhouettes that move at the will of mechanisms we do not understand. What strikes the reader more than anything is the perfection of the mechanism, which operates like a piece of clockwork, and by which, in the course of a moment-by-moment annotation of gestures and actions, the author succeeds in creating a continuum which itself acts as an interrogation of the narrative. It is neither the chronology of human actions, nor that of clocks, but the chronology of Robbe-Grillet himself. And the action plays so great a role that the work turns into a sort of detective novel. *Les Gommes* signalled the presence of a new and vigorous talent, but not a new novel-form. It was after the publication of this novel that the author and Roland Barthes began to theorize.

In *Le Voyeur*, 1955, the action is fragmented into a multiplicity of gestures and patterns of behaviour which seem to be intended to divert our attention from some event of major importance: the murder of a little shepherd-girl by the commercial traveller, whose comings and goings are meticulously timed before and after the supposed event. If this action had not been hidden from us, there would have been no novel. It is precisely the description of the efforts made by the murderer to fill in a gap of a few minutes in his timetable, to restore to the world, whose order has been seriously upset by his act, its smooth, 'intact' surface. Things, objects seem to be there to give him something to hold on to, to *distract* him. The solidity, the immutability of the universe help him to efface his criminal intervention, by relieving him of responsibility and investing him with this innocence. Not being a simple component of the universe he wishes to become one, effacing himself in the world in order to become, like the world, definable by what its 'surface' shows, that is, its gestures and behaviour. What would have been left if the murder had been described in the same way as the character's other actions? Is it not a simple trick of construction, on the part of the author, to have hidden it from us?

With *La Jalousie*, 1957, Robbe-Grillet abandons altogether both story and coherent, or even clearly recognizable characters. He presents us with a kaleidoscope of actions, or rather *visions* of actions (real or imaginary) which are jumbled together with no sense of passing time. Individuals are defined by their simple relations with each other – a husband, a wife, her lover – or with their environment – a nameless colony. In order to fill these gaps and voids, the author sets about, rule in hand, to make a geometrical description of places, objects, their position, the course of the sun and the shadows at different times in the day, repeating interminably the same descriptions, the same incidents, the same gestures and the same words. The effect is very strange: it is as if one has been transported into a shadow theatre in which only the scenery and the scene-shifters really exist, and in which, according to the very incomplete directions we are given, we are expected to participate. The solid world of objects seems to be the result of a vision, or a hallucination, and if the facts and events lack that 'depth' that the author denies to them, they also lack qualities that would make their existence credible. The extreme pursuit of objectivity is confused with the worst subjectivity: we see the world through the eyes of a jealous husband. This might even be its entire construction.

We must not conclude from this that Robbe-Grillet does not know what he is about, or that he has failed to create the world that he set out to create, or that his instrument has proved inadequate. The conquest of objectivity is an illusion, in so far as we use a language which cannot be that of things, which are by definition dumb. It is a human language: moreover, it is the novelist's language. In calling his novel *La Jalousie,* which denotes both an object and a feeling, the author condemns himself, without even admitting it, to showing us a jealous man and a world seen through the slats of a blind. The full world of which Robbe-Grillet draws up his inventory is, in fact, an empty world, devoid of meaning until man brings to it the complex relationships and dialectics that make of it a human world, even at the point at which an individual wishes to be absorbed into the world of things and objects. This wish to disappear, to be absorbed, also springs from subjectivity.

Overwhelming proof of this was to be found in *Dans le Labyrinthe*, 1959, which, by the trick of a maniacal description, turns everything into a hallucination. A soldier, asked by one of his dead comrades to take a box of letters and possessions of no more than sentimental value to his parents, wanders in the streets of a dead, snow-covered town whose houses all look alike. Street-lamps, doorways, corridors and stairs – all these things no doubt exist, but they do so like the disturbing objects painted by the surrealists which add to the unreality of the painting. In confining himself to creating images, and nothing but images, which, instead of succeeding each other, associate, combine, collide, jostle and merge together, the author blurs the reality that these images are supposed to be expressing, knocks away the support that reality was providing for them. What is the role here of the objective inventory, of dream and of hallucination? The reader is placed before a complex of mirrors, no doubt real in themselves, which project images but do not produce them. Robbe-Grillet achieves a result which is the exact opposite of the one that his theory set out to produce. This defeat of a controversial theoretician is the victory of a novelist. Robbe-Grillet has finally admitted that objectivity and subjectivity form the two complementary sides of his apprehension of the world and that the excess of one could be transformed into the other.

Nathalie Sarraute

Unlike Robbe-Grillet, Nathalie Sarraute has placed herself avowedly in the development of the novel-form. Learning much from the example of Dostoyevsky, and more perhaps from Virginia Woolf, she has tried to carry that development to its ultimate consequences.

Portrait d'un Inconnu, 1949, and *Martereau,* 1953, are novels devoid of any story, let alone plot, and the human beings that move in them – a grandfather, his granddaughter, or someone called Martereau – do not even possess individual boundaries. Nathalie Sarraute describes the movements of living forces, appetites, desires, which collide, unite and divide like those organic beings at the lower reaches of the animal scale which contract under the action of an acid or send out their pseudopodia. Her first work, *Tropismes,* which was published in 1936 and went practically unnoticed, bore even in this respect a significant title. It depicts human beings in groups (women chattering in a tea shop, passers-by looking into shop windows) who are moved by the various tiny shocks that come from the place, the circumstances, the situation. When individuals appear on the scene, they bear no resemblance to a type, but rather to a species at once zoological and social which is sufficient definition of them. She depicts a humanity of commonplaces.

Unlike Robbe-Grillet, who tries to remain at the surface of the world and wishes to confine himself to describing it, Nathalie Sarraute suggests the existence, beneath the banal appearances, of an 'underworld' of frenetic and swarming life which she believes to be the real world of human relations. It is this that forms the tissue of the novel, so that, speech having been given to man in order to disguise his thought, there exists beneath the surface of communication a 'sub-conversation' (gestures that contradict the words said, silences, *sous-entendus,* inflexions, positions, facial expressions), which is true communication. Far from limiting oneself to appearances, it is these appearances that must be penetrated and whose real meaning and lines of force must be shown. By such an analysis, Nathalie Sarraute reaches down to the springs of an elemental but complex life in which are born the elaborate forms of feelings, the efflorescences of 'psychology'. For her, not only do men not act according to reason or their principles: they have not even succeeded in conquering their individuality. What interests her is the common tissue of their existence, the gross relations (of adaptation, aggressivity, defence), or the subtle and inexpressible relations they have with the world and between themselves. The scale of these relations is as wide and diversified as the scale of human situations in which they operate.

In *Le Planétarium,* 1959, her most brilliant book, this 'underworld' is best seen under its metaphoric aspects, and the individuals are more distinguishable. The characters are recognizable: a young fool who imagines he has artistic tastes, a fussy aunt, a divided family, and even a typical well-known woman writer, who is seen both in her moments of glory and as an object of ridicule. These characters are in no way important, no more than the insignificant plot that serves as a thread holding the book together. What the author wishes to suggest by the very title of her novel is that each of these individuals moves, autonomous and enclosed, inside a system in which they attract, repel and strike each other, generally with great violence. The autonomous particle very rarely takes up a fixed position. What characterizes it is rather its capacity for display, retraction, bristling, elasticity and the rebuilding of cells destroyed by the enemy. This world of violent, lethal combat is also a closed, unbreakable world. We exist only for ourselves, and those of our opinions that seem most reasonable, concerning, for example, an immovable object, a work of art (see *Les Fruits d'Or*, 1963) are at the mercy of every variation in fashion and snobbery.

Michel Butor

The name of Michel Butor has long been linked with that of Robbe-Grillet. These two young novelists have nothing in common, however, and Michel Butor was the first to make this clear when he made a violent attack on the theories of the author of *Le Voyeur*. He too wishes to renovate the form, he too places great importance on the 'objective world' and has little use for 'psychology', but he does believe in his characters and in their relations with the world. For him, it is rather the world that has changed, notably in its two principal categories, space and time.

Unlike the other practitioners of the new novel, Butor does not believe that time can be got rid of quite so easily, either by mixing its tenses or by replacing it, as does Robbe-Grillet in *La Jalousie,* by an immobilized time. If time is a reality of the world as well as our own reality, this reality is not self-evident, it is not a fixed standard, as in the traditional novel. It has constantly to be recaptured, reconstructed, it is not to engulf the events we have experienced and our own personalities. Moreover, time is not just a simple container: it is woven into the very fibres of our being, which is manifested through its modes, in a dialectical relationship of which the antithesis is the manifestation of time through us. It is this 'Being-Time' complex that Michel Butor is striving to express, partly in the form of the Faulknerian 'chronicle', but also by a quite different technique: meticulous analysis in the description of details, rather than total and synthetic description.

In *L'Emploi du Temps,* 1956, the hero, who is both the narrator and the author, tries to write down, seven months after they took place, the events of his life in the English town of Bleston, where he is still staying at the time he starts trying to reconstruct them. The difficulty of this project lies in the fact that, at the time of writing, he continues to experience other events. It is particularly difficult to extricate himself from these events, as they are the consequences of the earlier events being described. As a result, the present is constantly breaking into the past, altering its content and tone, giving it a meaning that was not apparent at the time. What kind of solidity and permanence can be attributed to a reality that changes according to the moment at which one considers it? Doubt is cast upon the true nature of reality. The 'objective world', to which the narrator clings as the one thing that is safe and solid, itself becomes questionable, hallucinatory, evanescent. The attempt to reconquer time is an impossible one and the novel itself is proof of its failure: it is brought to an end, 'unfinished', by a dramatic recapitulation which is no more than a desperate attempt to finish the story off, and which indicates the impossibility of doing so.

La Modification, 1957, provides a striking innovation in form: the entire narrative is described in the vocative (*vous,* the polite form of the second person), but the content of the story is traditional. It concerns the slow, internal transformation of a man who, on the way to Rome to join his mistress, decides to leave things as they are, to stay with his wife and children, continue working as a commercial traveller, and spend his visits to Rome with his mistress. When he had got on the train, he had been imagining the full, carefree new life that lay before him. During the journey, his observations, thoughts, memories, even his dreams, which form of past and present a confused medley of events that jostle together, recur, overlap, have imperceptibly led him to 'modify' his plans. A whole life is revealed in a confusion of time and place, in which even the presence of the narrator is not always certain. The success of the work is due to the mastery with which this confusion is made intelligible. By the use of *vous,* the author also succeeds in modifying the traditional relationship of the novelist with his work. The use of this second person places a kind of juridical 'distance' between himself and what he relates, without allowing him to fall into the fallacious objectivity of the divinely omniscient narrator.

Degrés, 1960, is an even more ambitious work. More overtly than in his previous novels, Michel Butor tried to construct 'a totality within a description', even if this necessitated the most banal description imaginable. It consists of an exhaustive account, by a history and geography teacher, of one hour's lesson, on Tuesday, 12th October 1954. It contains not only an account of the lesson itself, but the entire life of the teacher, of the nephew to whom the account is addressed, of the school in which he teaches, of his family and his activities outside school, and of the actions and gestures of some of the thirty-two pupils in his class and of his colleagues. As the description grows, as detail is added to detail, the attempt to seize the whole of reality ends by effacing this reality, and we are left with nothing but a mass of notes, as in a diary. Each reader reads what he wishes into the book, according to his personal interests, and the totality of significance to which the novelist wishes to attain is lost in a total absence of significance. But here, too, it was probably the author's intention to show how any such attempt was doomed to failure: the book itself is proof of it.

Mobile, 1962, is also based upon the themes of time and space, but on a different scale, that of the American continent. The very immensity of the country, the rapid changes in time as one goes from east to west, and vice versa, the repetition to saturation point of the same, unvarying, monotonous human spectacle, combine to form an image of an incredibly inhuman reality that must come as a shock to a reader who is used to more familiar territory. He does not accept this sudden removal from his natural element to one so strange that he no longer has any sense of direction. He accuses the author of artifice, whereas the author has tried with the simplest possible means to convey a 'natural' vision.

In *Réseau Aérien*, 1962, Michel Butor, conscious of the extent to which the aeroplane has changed our view of the world and the rhythm of life, creates an image of this new world of space and time to which we must habituate ourselves.

Claude Simon

Claude Simon began his literary career after the Liberation with a traditional novel, *Le Tricheur,* whose hero is very close to Meursault in *L'Etranger.* But there is no question of direct influence. Simon expresses through his hero not so much the impossibility of taking an absurd world seriously as a difficulty in living at all. After some years of self-searching and silence, he wrote *Gulliver* and *Le Sacre du Printemps,* in which obsessive material breaks through the traditional narrative style that is imposed upon it. The rhythm is a syncopated one. A number of separate stories interweave and overlap. One feels that the author has read Faulkner and that he has learnt something from his reading. He appears in his own guise in *Le Vent*, 1957, and *L'Herbe*, 1958.

Le Vent, or '*tentative de restitution d'un retable baroque*', as it is sub-titled, takes us into a world of magic. Time is abolished, people's words and gestures seem to be frozen into some thick substance and the characters themselves are presented like static 'figures'. A rather laboured plot tells at great length of the various phases in the revolt of a Dostoyevsky-like 'innocent' against a constantly aggressive world. She loses herself in the matter of experienced time. There is no progress, only a feeling of constant reiteration, which is aided by a weighty prose, overloaded with participles and adjectives, rather like cement. The author is trying not so much to interest or move the reader as to hypnotize him. He succeeds when the reader succeeds in breaking through the barrier of the writing or himself sinks into the viscous element of the prose.

L'Herbe, 1958, invokes a quotation from Pasternak: 'Nobody makes history; it cannot be seen, any more than grass can be seen growing.' By history, Simon means here both human history, which, as in all Claude Simon's novels, is fatalistic, and fictional narrative. The characters of *L'Herbe* (an old woman who is dying, her niece, and the niece's husband and lover) have, in fact, no history, or at least one so banal as not to be worth mentioning. What interests the author is the material that can be extracted from the events of a life; and again, it is this matter that he makes so fascinating. His unimportant, scarcely distinguishable characters take on a relief that no analysis could have given them. The whole construction of the novel forms a block in which we are made prisoners.

La Route des Flandres, 1961, links even more closely the general history of mankind (the defeat of 1940), the history of a family and the stories of individuals. They interact by means of actions in the present, giving rise to memories, visions and hallucinations. In a tightly-woven material formed of time and space, with many 'holes' and 'patches', individuals are caught like spiders in their webs and move about like insects. Yet each individual carries about him a boundless world which intersects with other worlds. It is enough for him simply to live, and it is this life, merging with others, taken up by the vast movement of the world, tossed about at the mercy of events, sinking into memory or spreading out over the surface of things, that Claude Simon has striven to express in words, in a language dense and obscure.

He succeeds once more in *Le Palace*, 1962, which recounts an episode in the Spanish Civil War – at least, it appears to. It is not so much an actual event – the assassination of a revolutionary leader by enemies on his own side – that the author evokes, as the particular atmosphere of a revolutionary headquarters, of a town (Barcelona), of an angry people, with its smells, its heat, its street-scenes. Claude Simon makes brilliant use of his heavily-weighted, meandering, serpentine sentence. Imperceptibly it has become for him an instrument of discovery and creation. It passes over reality like a sponge, sucking it dry.

Claude Ollier

Although *La Mise en Scène* appeared after *Les Gommes* and *Le Voyeur*, it is said that Claude Ollier preceded Robbe-Grillet in discovering the aesthetic system which aims at expressing the world in its total objectivity. He is also more systematic, more radical than Robbe-Grillet.

In *La Mise en Scène*, which describes a tropical expedition, the world is a décor, man an insect whose behaviour belongs to entomology. With minute care for detail, the author describes the gestures, the actions, reports the speech, recounts the events that the reader needs to recreate the whole. It is not a puzzle, since all the constituents of the construction are already connected by the narrative. The author is no more present in this narrative than in what he presents to our view and records like a machine. He wishes to be and is, in fact, pure vision.

What is seen and heard is transmitted, through the work, in its total objectivity. But how can the work remain objective when another eye, the reader's, takes over, selecting, separating the accidental from the essential, rearranging, evaluating, when another consciousness in search of a meaning takes the place of the author's? No doubt this is the result of bad habits of mind, which, unfortunately, we cannot escape. One can imagine therefore that, depending on the reader, the work can be interpreted in the most different ways, and that what seems to one a simple account can take on for another the colours of fantasy. But at least Claude Ollier has broken with the conception of narrative as possessing only those meanings that the author chooses to give it. Like any other fact in the novel, the creation of the novelist is open to any interpretation.

That meticulous, even fanatical description of reality can plunge, like dreams, into unreality, is proved by *Le Maintien de l'Ordre*, 1962, which seems to be about nothing more than the observation by two men of a third whom they want to kill. Despite the author, an atmosphere is created that is more and more enveloping, an action develops that has all the surprises of a thriller, our interest is aroused in characters however little we know of their motives, in short, a reality takes shape before our eyes which probably has little connection with the one that has been so minutely described to us. With a freedom that has never before been offered so generously to the reader, we collaborate with the novelist in the construction of his story. Total impersonality meets, through the reader, total subjectivity. A world uniformly flat discovers its hills and valleys: the bark of reality, the skin of things, is no more than a thin membrane that is only too easy to penetrate. Claude Ollier's obstinate determination to reach the end of the road he alone had taken has led him to a point at which opposites become interchangeable and contradictions become equal and cancel each other out.

Robert Pinget

Robert Pinget did not at first wish to become a novelist. He began by publishing a number of ironical, satirical tales which had no moral (*Mahu ou le Matériau,* 1952, *Le Renard et la Boussole,* 1953). His talent becomes surer, and more deliciously disconcerting, in *Graal Flibuste,* 1957. It tells the story of an imaginary voyage to an imaginary country peopled by imaginary beings. It is reminiscent of the inventions of an Henri Michaux who wished to be satirical rather than cruel and who was not above using linguistic games.

Baga, 1958, has a more coherent story and its inventiveness is less linguistic. Baga exists as a king while ever he fulfils that office. He exists as a man when he becomes a hermit in the middle of a forest. Fantasy is given full rein. Overflowing with words, it is sometimes lacking in rigour and weight.

Le Fiston, 1959, is a real novel and even a 'new novel'. It is the story of a father writing to his son, asking him to come home. To lure him back, he recounts all the events that occur in the village, from love affairs to funerals, as if to create a vision of a life so rich that the son might be tempted to return. The father is also a drunkard, who is constantly beginning his letter again. The same events are never described in the same way: an imperceptible and subtle discrepancy makes them no more than possible; they might even be invented. Robert Pinget has finally discovered his own way of destroying reality.

He uses this method in *L'Inquisitoire,* 1962, in which a deaf old man gives the wrong answers to questions asked him by a policeman concerning a crime of which he might have been a witness. By the play of question and answer, a strange, phantasmagorical world, that is at the same time oddly Balzacian, as precise as an inventory, is created before us, in all its strange, tragic, incongruous detail. One could almost describe the geography, the topography of this world. Yet it has no more than a possible existence, it is only the vision of a deaf old man immured in his own stories. The monumental, baroque edifice that the novelist has constructed is no sounder or more firmly based than a house of cards.

15 *The Future of the Novel*

For the past twenty years, the sickness of the novel has been a constant subject of debate. Specialists have been called to its bedside, its pulse has been taken, it has been examined and all kinds of treatment advocated. For some, the novel is dying; for others, it is dead; others again consider that it is reviving and about to enjoy a second youth. Apart from remarking that it was in a similar state at the beginning of the century, two things must be said at once: the form has never flourished so obviously as it does today, at least in quantity, and, for the writer, the novel remains his favourite form of expression. Sensitive to every current of ideas, expressing all modes of feeling, adapting itself to any situation demanded of it and subject to all kinds of circumstances, the novel can truly be considered to be the thermometer of society. It expresses ways of reacting to events, of thinking and of feeling common to all; it provides material for philosophers, historians and sociologists. The 'sickness' of the novel is none other than that of the social environment. When the novel is ill, society is not in a healthy state.

It is also, and is above all, a personal creation. It expresses the particular way in which one man, the novelist, reacts to the world and acts upon it. Whatever school or movement it may belong to, whatever theory it may put into practice, or whatever techniques it employs, the novel is worth no more than the novelist. The greater or deeper the novelist's conceptions are, the sharper his sensibility, the more perfected his means of expression, the more the result at which he aims will be capable of moving others, either in scope or intensity, the more too it will manifest, in some particular and special way, a totality which, through him, takes on form and meaning. All forms of literary expression can find a place in the novel and the novel embraces them all. If new forms, more suited to as yet unimagined societies or to unexpected modes of feeling, develop, it would be surprising if the novel did not, in due course, absorb them.

Can the cinema, audio-visual techniques and other media of communication founded on new discoveries make the novel die of inanition or suddenly shorten its days of life? The answer does not lie in the future, but in the past, where it was believed that photography and the cinema would replace painting and the theatre. One means of expression can be added to others without necessarily destroying them. On the contrary, it encourages them to enrich and transform themselves. Confronted with techniques based upon strong forms of aggression which are no longer at the stage (attained by all art) of seeking the active participation of the listener or spectator, and which, on the contrary, treat him very often as an object, the novel expresses an obstinate reality which does not easily allow itself to be circumvented. Only the novelist can explore its labyrinths, only he can sound its depths. He is bound by an enterprise that the reader must carry through with him, and which becomes the common property of both. He creates his readers just as they give him life. Only the word (or the image) treated as an end and not as a means allows communication to be established at the right level.

Reportage, the documentary, the description of real events, even the confession, do not possess the virtues of the novel. Impressive as accounts of the war, with all its atrocities, or of the life in concentration camps were, they could not have provided a true image if they had not been sustained by the works of David Rousset, Robert Antelme, Jean Cayrol and Louis Martin-Chauffier. The naked horror was striking, but it did not speak. It did not say that men, whom others had attempted to destroy in what made them essentially men, did in fact win, if only intermittently and in a small number of cases, the tragic struggle in which they were engaged. It failed to say the very thing that mattered most.

The novel is based upon a combination of knowledge, experience and meditation which it transmutes into a total vision that knowledge, experience and meditation alone cannot provide.

One can assemble all the images of an absurd world yet fail to achieve the image of the absurdity of the world as it exists in *L'Etranger*. And the existentialist novel has done more than the theoretical works of Sartre to persuade us that we were wrong to believe in the permanence of the world or of consciousness. After having seen executioners and victims, profiteers and exploited, *salauds* and innocents, we are convinced that there cannot be a 'human nature' of which each individual is the possessor and incarnation from birth. Beliefs, values and moral systems are judged according to the way they are practised. What other form of communication could be more persuasive and of more help? The novel always retains the mask of a revelation about ourselves, made by ourselves, in close co-operation with the novelist who discovers it for us.

The reaction that marked the fifties seemed to end a period in which the novelist had tended to be eclipsed by the philosopher, the 'committed' writer, the responsible intellectual. We witnessed a return in strength of the traditional novel of entertainment, as practised by talented writers who wished to mask the fish in a sauce of 'fine writing', to imprison an anarchistic and suicidal revolt in less disturbing forms and to end what appeared to them to be pedantic and boring. They were unable to disguise the anxiety that corroded their choice of gratuitousness, elegance and humour: they fell into frivolity. Words used to distract man from his torment lost their value and the novel could not be considered simply as a department of the art of writing.

The novel has become 'total', drawing for its needs upon anything, even techniques that would take its place and whose methods it deliberately adopts. It bursts its bonds. When man and the world are brought into question, how could this question be presented within a fixed form? Georges Bataille does not write 'novels', and it is extremely difficult to label work in which fiction, poetry, wandering meditation and illumination are mingled together. Can it be said of Maurice Blanchot that he writes, on the one hand, critical studies and, on the other, novels, when *L'Attente, L'Oubli* belong to neither category? When either Genet or Sartre confide the fate of their words to actors or enclose them between the pages of a book, they are of the same nature. It is the same with Samuel Beckett who asks only the minimum of help from fiction: plot, setting and characters serve as guides through an almost anonymous language that draws its strength from itself alone. Literature itself, and with it the novel, is now brought into question. Yet to deny language with language is not to enclose oneself within a vicious circle. Language is language, but it is also what transcends it: that tongue of fire from which it springs and which constitutes its 'beyond'. It is this that the novelist tries to communicate.

The practitioners of the 'new novel' have reconciled themselves to the novel. For them, it condemns itself as a form of expression, a literary *genre,* as a particular use of language. Is it possible to fall into so obvious a trap? We move quite consciously in the world of 'as if'. Not everything is simply reflection and illusion. Time, space, consciousness, either crushed together or smashed into fragments, do not result in chaos. They are organized according to the grand laws of the mind which, as a result, take on a new content and a new appearance. They are arranged in an approximation that is closer to life. The whole of this difficult way through chaos and ruins leads us to what we are, to what the world is around us. It enables us not to continue living as strangers in our own lives.

If the novel is moving in this direction, it is useless to concern ourselves with its future. One can break down the barriers, retreat into old forms, invent new ones, place the *genre* in doubt or literature itself in question, deny reality, aspire to silence and nothingness, all these deformations, negations and rebirths become flesh in a 'fable' which we need because it is addressed to the whole of the human complex, on every level, from everyday reality to myth. It will last as long as men have recourse to metaphors in order to explain to themselves their presence in the world.

APPENDIX

A Selection of Critical Texts

Looking back on the Concentration Camps

JEAN CAYROL

There is nothing to explain. The victims of the concentration camps suffered their experiences in different ways. Some of them are now dead, others are slowly dying, cut off from the return road, growing old in the larva-like cast of a fear only half extinguished; many are alive, attempting to make a way for themselves through the Intangible Camp which, once again, surrounds them, holds them spellbound and will not let them rest. The emotional shock remains stronger than ever, with whiffs from that extreme of misery finding their way even into the most hidden corners of peace: the smell of the concentration camp is stronger than ever. And those who have known the camps only at second hand are beginning to adopt the more noticeable tics of that world. If today the mangled body turned up by the ploughshare is kicked out of the way, if one keeps silent so as to give each individual the opportunity of being a man, it is no less true that the influence, the solicitude of the concentration camp are constantly spreading, not only in their uninterrupted manifestations (one can imagine new maps in which the principalities of Murder are marked out for the next 'explorers' of these lands of desolation), but also in the psyche of Europe, even of the world.

The Literature which is ending its life in the last twitchings of a ruined intellectual capitalism has never enough material for all those writers, known and unknown. Perhaps it too could be given a new lease of life by its close contact with this demoniacal effervescence. Perhaps it might in some way provide the first sketches for a new 'concentrationary' novel, creating the characters for a new Inhuman Comedy, for, to use a fashionable word, a 'concentrationary' *realism* that would find its way into each scene of our private lives.

I must admit at once to a certain mistrust, certain misgivings before a spiritual quest in which the foundations of traditional psychology would be so profoundly shaken; but one cannot ignore the ascendance that the concentration camp appears to have over our minds, the hypnotic power it seems to possess over so many nations. Our immediate future is beginning to feel its first manifestations and give birth to its strange cohorts. There is no myth of the concentration camp; there is a 'concentrationary' reality in everyday life.

It seems to me to be time that we bore witness to these strange advances of the 'concentrationary' world, to its first hesitant attacks on the world in which we live. They are the result of a great fear and they bear its stigmata.

In any case, it is not absurd to envisage an Art born directly from such a human convulsion, from a catastrophe which has shaken the very foundations of our consciousness, an Art that could be so little affected by the blackmail exercised by all literary fashion, an Art which, because of its creations and even its techniques, would be called 'Lazarian' art. It already exists in outline in our literary history (it would be easy to discover a diurnal and a nocturnal side in its development).

And this Art whose nature is exceptional and profoundly disturbing, in which the incredible and the natural merge into each other, is basically, in its paroxysm, only one of the very ordinary aspects that gradually, unknown to us, would characterize new works, not only of literature, but of Art in general, in painting and in music. One can foresee, and it is already perceptible in the work of certain young painters, a 'concentrationary' or 'Lazarian' influence (the continual repetition of the same formulas, the hypnotic state of forms and volumes, a certain tension of colour, a panic world of objects, etc.); the line refuses to bend to the demands of the wound, to take on its sinuosity and hesitancy. Picasso is the painter above all who could have set up his easel on the Appelplatz of Mauthausen or Buchenwald. We are going through an uncertain period in contemporary painting in which anything can happen, degenerate or change without the painter knowing what hand guides his brush or what terrified vision takes over his sight.

In literature, the influence is less insistent, more restrained, the writer continues to believe in the dogmas of a Stendhal or a Balzac; he knows what is to be found even behind the most securely locked doors. He feels at ease in fiction, unlike some who, growing ever more anxious at not seeing names written on the doors, go out armed. Today we are awaiting the arrival of warrior-writers, men who will not be ashamed to stride over corpses and decay and to whom, I am sure, the gates of the Kingdom of God will be opened; we have need more than ever before of writers of 'public safety', who would not be afraid of dirtying their hands, of descending into even the blackest of souls: the illustrious house of mankind. (. . .)

. . . It seems to me that it is already possible to distinguish some of the principles of a 'Lazarian' or 'concentrationary' Art and I believe it to be of prime importance to point them out, revealing all their marks, tearing away all masks, lest the disease spreads; nothing must be left in the dark, for the dark comes only too quickly.

This mysterious, subtle, still furtive Art can become in effect, if we continue to frequent charnel-houses of every kind – men being shot down in public places in China under the impassive eye of the camera – the only Art, inseparable from the precarious condition of man, an art which has already found perhaps its first historian and explorer in the anxious figure of Albert Camus. (. . .)

(From *Pour un romanesque lazaréen*, 1950)

Commitment

JEAN-PAUL SARTRE

La Fin de la Nuit is not a novel. How can anyone call this angular, glacial book, with its analyses, theatrical passages and poetic meditations a 'novel'? How can anyone confuse these bursts of speed and violent jamming of the brakes, these abrupt starts and breakdowns, with the majestic flow of fictional time? How can anyone be taken in by this motionless narrative, which betrays its intellectual framework from the very start, in which the mute faces of the heroes are inscribed like angles in a circle? If it is true that a novel is a *thing,* like a painting or architectural structure, if it is true that a novel is made with time and free minds, as a picture is painted with oil and pigments, then *La Fin de la Nuit* is not a novel. It is, at most, a collection of signs and intentions. M. Mauriac is not a novelist.

Why? Why hasn't this serious and earnest writer achieved his purpose? Because, I think, of the sin of pride. Like most of our writers, he has tried to ignore the fact that the theory of relativity applies in full to the universe of fiction, that there is no more place for a privileged observer in a real novel than in the world of Einstein, and that it is no more possible to conduct an experiment in a fictional system in order to determine whether the system is in motion or at rest than there is in a physical system. M. Mauriac has put himself first. He has chosen divine omniscience and omnipotence. But novels are written *by* men and *for* men. In the eyes of God, Who cuts through appearances and goes beyond them, there is no novel, no art, for art thrives on appearances. God is not an artist. Neither is M. Mauriac.

(From 'M. François Mauriac et la Liberté', 1939, *Situations, I*, 1947, translated by Annette Michelson as 'François Mauriac and Freedom' in *Literary and Philosophical Essays, 1955*)

All writers of bourgeois origin have known the temptation of irresponsibility: for a century now, it has been a traditional characteristic of a literary career. The author merely establishes a connection between his work and the money it brings him. On the one hand, he writes, sings, sighs; on the other, he is given money. Here are two apparently unconnected facts; the best he can do is to tell himself that he is being kept for his sighing. He considers himself to be more like a student with a grant than a worker who receives the price of his labour. The theoreticians both of Art for Art's Sake and of Realism have confirmed him in this opinion of himself. Has anyone noticed that they both have the same aims and the same origins? The main concern of the writer who follows the teaching of the first is to produce useless works; if they really are gratuitous, without any apparent connection with the world, then they are not far from seeming beautiful to him. So he places himself outside society, or rather he will not consent to appear in society merely as a simple consumer: just like the student. The Realist, too, is a consumer. But production is another matter: he has been told that science has no concern for its utility, so he aims at the dry impartiality of the scientist. We have been told often enough that he 'looked down at' the environments he wished to describe. Looked down at! Where was he, then? In the air? The truth is that, uncertain of his social position, too timorous to oppose the bourgeoisie that paid him, too lucid to accept it without reservations, he chose to judge his century, convincing himself that in this way he would remain outside it, as the research scientist is outside his field of research. Thus the distinterestedness of pure science links up with the gratuitousness of Art for Art's Sake. It is not by chance that Flaubert is both pure stylist, pure lover of form and the father of naturalism; it is no accident that the brothers Goncourt prided themselves both on knowing how to observe and on being able to write like artists.

This inheritance of irresponsibility has troubled many minds. They suffer from a bad literary conscience and do not seem to know whether it is an admirable or a grotesque thing to write. The poet used to consider himself to be a prophet, which was honourable; then he became an outcast, a *maudit,* which was good enough. But today, he has fallen into the ranks of the specialists and it is not without a certain uneasiness that he writes 'man of letters' after his name in hotel visitors' books. Man of letters: this combination of words is itself enough to put one off writing; it makes one think of an Ariel, a Vestal, an *enfant terrible,* or a harmless madman who dabbles in weight-lifting or numismatics. This is quite ridiculous enough. The man of letters writes when others are fighting; one day he is proud to feel himself the priest and guardian of ideal values; next day, he finds to his shame that literature is more like some kind of perverted affection. Among the bourgeois who read him, he is conscious of his dignity; but among workers who do not read him, he suffers from an inferiority complex as was shown in 1936 at the Maison de la Culture. It is certainly this complex that lies at the origin of what Paulhan calls terrorism, it was this that led the surrealists to despise the very literature from which they lived. After the first war, a particular kind of lyricism was fashionable; the best writers, the purest ones, confessed publicly what was most humiliating for them, and appeared pleased when they had drawn the reprobation of the bourgeois upon themselves: they had produced a writing which, by its consequences, was rather like an action. Those isolated attempts could not prevent words being devalued every day. There was a crisis of rhetoric, then a crisis of language. At the outbreak of the last war, most writers had become resigned to being no more than nightingales. But then writers were found who wished to carry the disgust with literary creation to its extreme: going further than their elders, whom they considered not to have done enough in publishing a book that was simply useless, they maintained that the secret aim of all literature was the destruction of language and that it was enough to talk and say nothing for this aim to be achieved. This inexhaustible silence was fashionable for some time and Hachette distributed these pills of silence to their station bookstalls in the form of thick novels. Today things have reached the point at which one has seen writers show pained surprise when attacked or punished for having used their pens in the service of the Germans. 'So what?' they say. 'Am I committed personally by what I write?'

We do not wish to be ashamed of writing and we have no desire to talk and say nothing. Even if we had, we should not succeed in doing so: nobody can. All writing has a meaning, even if that meaning is far removed from what the author intended. For us, in fact, the writer is neither a Vestal, nor an Ariel: whatever he does, he is 'in the thick of it', he is marked, compromised, even in his farthest retreat. If, at certain times he uses his art to produce articles of sonorous inanity, even that is a sign: it means that there is a crisis in literature and, probably, in society, or that the ruling classes have deflected him, without him knowing, towards a luxury activity, for fear that he might swell the ranks of revolution. Flaubert, who inveighed so much against the bourgeoisie and who believed that he had withdrawn from the social machine, what is he now but a talented *rentier*? And does his meticulous art not imply the comfort of Croisset, the solicitude of a mother or niece, a régime of order, prosperous trade, and regular dividends? It does not require many years for a book to become a social fact that is used like an institution or entered like an object in statistics; it does not require much time for it to become part of the trappings of a whole period, with its dress, its hats, its methods of transport and its food. The historian will say of us: 'They ate this, they read that, they dressed like this.' The first railways, the cholera, the revolt of the silk-weavers of Lyons, the novels of Balzac, the development of industry are equally characteristic of the July Monarchy. All this has been said and repeated since Hegel: we wish to draw practical conclusions from it. Since the writer has no means of escape, we want him to become closely involved with his times; it is his only chance: they are made for him and he is made for them. One regrets Balzac's indifference before the Days of 48 and Flaubert's frightened incomprehension before the Commune; one regrets it for *their* sake: there was something they missed for ever. We do not want to miss anything in our own time: it may not be the finest, but it is our own; we have only *this* life to live, in the midst of *this* war or, perhaps, *this* revolution. Let it not be concluded from this that we are preaching a kind of popularism: quite the contrary. Popularism is the child of aged parents, the sad offspring of the last realists; it is yet another attempt to withdraw from the game. We are convinced on the contrary that one cannot *withdraw* from the game. If we were as dumb and silent as stones, our very passivity would be an action. For the author who devotes his life to writing novels about the Hittites, his absention is itself a taking up of position. The writer is a part of his period: every word has its echoes. Every silence too. I hold Flaubert and Goncourt responsible for the repression that followed the Commune because they did not write a line to prevent it. It was not their business, someone might say. But was the trial of Calas Voltaire's business? Was the condemnation of Dreyfus Zola's business? Was the administration of the Congo Gide's business? Each of these writers, at a particular stage in his life, weighed up his responsibilities as a writer. The Occupation taught us ours. Since we act upon our times by our very existence, we have chosen to make this action voluntary. It must be said again: it is not unusual for a writer to play his modest part in preparing the future. But there is a vague and conceptual future that concerns the whole of humanity and on which enlightenment can be found nowhere. Will history come to an end? Will the sun go out? What will be the condition of man in the socialist society of the year 3000? We leave these dreams to the writers of science fiction; it is the future of *our* period that must receive our attention: a limited future that is scarcely visible – for a period, like a man, is first of all a future. It is made up of its works in progress, its more or less long-term plans, its revolts, its struggles, its hopes: when will the war end? How will the country be reconstructed? How will international relations work out? What will be the social reforms? Will the forces of reaction triumph? Will there be a revolution and what will it be? We make this future ours, we do not want any other. Other writers, no doubt, have less pressing concerns and more far-reaching visions. They move among us like absentees. Where are they, then? With their great-nephews they have come back to judge that vanished period that was ours and of which we are the sole survivors. But their calculations are false: posthumous fame is always based upon a misunderstanding. What do they know of those nephews who will come among us to visit them! Immortality is a terrible alibi: it is not easy to live with one foot before and one foot beyond the grave. How can one deal with present-day affairs, when one is looking so far ahead! How can we raise enthusiasm for a battle or enjoy a victory? Everything is equivalent. They look at us without seeing us: we are already dead in their eyes – and they go back to the novel they are writing for men they will never see. They have lost their lives to immortality. We write for our contemporaries, we have no wish to see our world with the eyes of the future – that would be the surest way of killing ourselves – but with our eyes of flesh, with real, perishable eyes. We do not wish to win our trial by appeal and we need only a posthumous rehabilitation: it is just here, while we are alive, that trials are won and lost.

(From 'Présentation des "Temps Modernes"', 1945,
Situations, II, 1948)

The Reaction against Existentialism

JACQUES LAURENT

(. . .) Both equally proud of their university education, Sartre of having been a teacher and Bourget of presenting himself as a sort of doctor without a degree, both 'doctors in social science', they were from the start bubbling with ideas and ambitions to exploit them. But they are confused ideas. Whether they are preconceived or original, they are equally gratuitous, equally arrogant in the way they are affirmed without proof, equally loose in their logical structure.

The similarity of the two writers can be established therefore at the level of confused ideas which they felt to be far-reaching – providing, of course, that they could be developed far enough. In fact, such a development was impossible. Bourget, for example, had got it into his head that Kant's philosophy was diabolical and tended to lead young men to debauchery and crime. He knew perfectly well that this idea was without foundation, was completely unprovable, and that he could expect nothing but ridicule from an essay entitled: 'Reasons for which an intellectual, if he reads Kant, abuses a virgin and kills her.'

Sartre, for his part, also had his *idée fixe,* which was to explain – or to explicit, to use his own language – fascism by inversion. It was one of those nice little convictions, brilliant no doubt, but quite impervious either to logical demonstration or historical analysis. A typical Bourget idea. Like Bourget, Sartre finally realized that his essay 'Homosexuality considered as the preparatory stage to Fascism' would not perhaps be published in the collection *Une Œuvre, un Portrait* with illustrations by Dubuffet, and found himself faced once more by the problem with which we left Bourget.

The tragedy is that these problems were constantly repeated. Ideas continued to flow, but they were always of the same kind, impervious, that is, to reason. Thus Sartre discovered, without being able to explain more, that by each gesture a man committed the whole of humanity, that if he married he committed all mankind to the path of marriage. He even began to ask himself if, in preferring a coffee éclair to a chocolate éclair, a customer in a cake shop was not committing everybody else to coffee éclairs. He then became anxious to know if, after all, a man was anything other than what others saw in him. This was why he feared 'to be an object, that is to recognize myself in that degraded, dependent and petrified being that I am for others . . . I need the meditation of others to be what I am.' There must be a metaphysic, even a sociology, to be found here, since this discovery enables one to formulate assertions like this: 'A Jew is no more than a man whom other men call a Jew'; 'a thief is no more than a man whom other men call a thief'; and, finally, 'I am becoming a man whom other men call a writer'.

Among other Sartrean ideas, Bourget came up with some that resembled those of his pupil in their very content. He too had examined the case of others and had described the dilemma of the civilized man thus: 'He is a man for whom the consciousness of others exists and who cannot bear to be judged . . . he cannot retire into his own soul, alone with his own ideas . . . he needs the opinion of others.'

It also occurred to him that divorce was a crime against society, and that it needed two generations to raise someone from the working class to the bourgeoisie. Two, why not three, or one? It just was so.

It just was so, but Sartre and Bourget would have risked being dismissed as Sunday thinkers if they had been so imprudent as to try to justify such hastily conceived theories, that no amount of commitment or even sophism would have been able to support. (. . .)

... A pitiable reflection on the thinking and reasoning faculties of Sartre and Bourget. Here are two academics, both products of the Sorbonne, who seem incapable of thinking clearly and yet whose ambition it is to impose their ideas upon the general public. This is how the novel of ideas came about.

For the authors knew that their essays, 'Reasons for which an intellectual, if he reads Kant, abuses a virgin and kills her' and 'Of homosexuality considered as the preparatory stage to Fascism' would be laughed at by their publishers. There was too much literary competition for them to hope to make themselves heard, no matter how enthralling their jargon-ridden declamations may be. Before an essay, or a treatise, the reader is an examiner who agrees or who does not agree, but whose agreement must be obtained by good reasoning. If he is told that Julien Sorel has dark hair, he believes it without it having to be proved to him. He is even only too anxious to complete what the sketch of a character or the description of a place necessarily leave incomplete. One has only to offer him 'a radiant face' and this vague designation will draw from him a particular image. For the novelist, he is a collaborator throughout, and not a censor as he is for the essayist. From the fact that he himself participates in the novel, the reader soon becomes a partisan witness who, since he has collaborated in the development of the narrative, is in no position to exercise doubt.

Thus, rather than try to demonstrate the undemonstrable, Bourget presents us with a studious, intelligent boy who loves his mother. The reader sees this boy, adopts him and watches him grow up. When, thanks to us, he exists, the lad begins to read Kant and other bad masters. He then goes on to seduce and poison the daughter of the house in which he is tutor. Ah, well! We bow before the facts: we cannot do otherwise. Robert was a good child, who, as we remember, loved his mother. He read bad books, debauched a pure young woman and brought her to her death. So it must have been the fault of Kant. (. . .)

... Bourget's lesson did not pass unnoticed and half a century later Sartre succeeded in a masterly fashion in pulling off the same trick again. He was careful not to publish a treatise demonstrating the connection between inversion and Fascism. He leaves Lucien in *L'Enfance d'un Chef* and Daniel in *Les Chemins de la Liberté*, who are as docile in Sartre's hands as Robert Greslou in Bourget's, the task of presenting this illegitimate tandem. (...)

(From *Paul et Jean-Paul*, 1951)

Literary Morals

JULIEN GRACQ

(...) The Frenchman, on the contrary, judges his *class* by the way in which he talks about literature, and it is a subject on which he cannot bear to find himself at a loss: certain names thrown into the conversation are expected to stimulate an automatic reaction on his part, as if it were a question of his health or his personal affairs – for him it is a personal matter – it is one of those subjects on which it is unthinkable that he should not pass an opinion. Thus it is that in France literature is written and criticized against a noisy background that is to be found nowhere else, and from which it is doubtless inseparable: the clamour of an unstable and over-excited crowd, the feverish murmur of a perpetual Stock Exchange. And in fact – its exact volume and size are unimportant – this volatile public (Paris has always had its salons or its literary districts), like the members of the Stock Exchange, has the strange peculiarity of being almost constantly in a state of excitement: there is the same snatching up of news, which is absorbed everywhere simultaneously like water sinking into sand, amplified into rumour, coined into echoes, into the gossip of the corridors – the same edginess, even the same feminine instability in one's reactions – the same need to have one's state of excitation continually stimulated by the *new* – the same light-headed frenzy to interpret whatever turns up: not a single book or a single author is thrown as fodder to this crowd, but it is worked upon by a kind of leaven, computed, dissected, interpreted, sounded, prolonged already into an imaginary future, evaluated from every possible point of view. Contact with this over-stimulated and over-stimulating public, whose pulse beats slightly above normal – a contact that is not easily forgotten – does not leave the writer unaffected. For a foreign writer, the public consists of little anonymous lamps that are quietly lit after dinner, something like the bucolic image of peaceful, uneventful rumination in the country – for the French writers it is a drug that is constantly within reach. (Once a French writer has published a book, he never ceases to write, as long as he is capable of doing so, any more than an actor ceases to act; we have still not got over the Rimbaud scandal – in America, on the contrary, nobody is surprised if a writer changes his job.) From this perpetual clash of opinion there results an adulteration, an alienation even of its taste of which the public is often only half conscious. From the moment one agrees to discuss one's personal preferences – and that in a country in which, ever since it existed, it has been customary for literature to refer itself to certain type-values that it reveres, but which it has not itself created (for centuries French literature considered itself to be an epigone of the ancient classics and this has left its mark) – there is in their expression an excess of singularity that is no longer acceptable. The corners are rounded off. If, by arguing from a simple, felt preference, I state for example (as I do) that I would give almost the whole of the literature of the last ten years for a single, little-known book by Ernst Jünger, *Sur les Falaises de Marbre,* or that the only French novel that has really interested me since the Liberation is an obscure work by Robert Margerit, *Mont Dragon* – and I am tired of repeating it – it is considered tolerable that I should say this once or twice to amuse myself or to be 'provocative', but if I go on saying it I am written off as a 'difficult' person. In the end, a kind of dullness is produced, by omission. One can imagine what would happen if a man accidentally perceived ultra-violet or infra-red rays – he would soon be persuaded to shut his eyes for his own safety. After all, there are more serious causes to take up than literary ones. When one witnesses a literary conversation, without, for once, taking part, without joining the game, one feels, with a slight feeling of vertigo, that one is observing people who are for the most part *Daltonians,* practising a kind of 'make-believe': they talk, they talk incessantly of things that they literally do not even perceive, that they will never perceive; they create a kind of immunizing representation, with that flair peculiar to the blind: they can *move around* things, and the conversation wanders comfortably between precipices, like a somnambulist on the edge of a roof. One must speak out and make oneself heard at all costs; one cannot escape it: the French public does not, like foreigners, see itself as a collection of inoffensive citizens who share a common 'hobby', but who each selects his own favourite fishing haunt without troubling the others – it sees itself rather as an electoral college in which the vote is obligatory, and in which each writer or book of note gives rise, by its very appearance, to a perpetual referendum. While others rummage among the mass of published material for food that suits their stomachs, the French public knows that it is destined from birth to elect the Presidents of the Republic of Letters. It is this parliamentary kitchen, these jealousies, these harem intrigues, these corridor manœuvres, these corruptions, these second ballots, more Machiavellian than those of the Most Serene Republic, this *cursus honorum* full of traps and détours, that make French literary life so basely exciting. For the French writer seems to believe that he exists not so much because people read him, but because he is talked about. He must constantly prod a press – that is only too apt to slumber (and not so much the critics as the gossip-columnists, who provide the supreme reward) – tongues must be kept wagging. An anxious, breathless 'Here I am! Here I am! I am still here!' is sometimes the only pathetic message to be read, by the experienced eye, between the lines of some famous writer, whose book one idly picks up, hoping that the dust is not too thick. Yet there is nothing there, at least it is not necessarily that he no longer has anything to say to us; but it is his *book of the year*: the public must once more take note of him, lest he be forgotten. In this rue Quincampoix, where our literary shares are marked up or down each day, whether he is in good health or poor, nothing means more to him than the feeling that he is one of those key names whose ups and downs affect the whole market – and to this demanding – and ruinous – feeling of being carried on the crest of a wave, one knows careers that have sacrificed everything. (. . .)

. . . The gap between the reputation accorded to an author and the sum total of real and enlightened devotion he inspires translates this fact of contemporary observation: that in literary matters there are more people in France than anywhere else who 'repeat what the papers say'. So long as the gap observed does not exceed certain limits, it would be wrong to take offence: it is a sign, after all, that literature is in a healthy state, like a political party that wishes to increase the circulation of its newspaper and enlarge its halo of sympathizers: similarly, no great writer has really felt wronged by the respect that the public has for the Académie. But the situation is gloomy indeed when, on the contrary, as is the case in this mid-point of the century, credit circulation begins to exceed, in an exaggerated way, the cash balance, that is, when opinions expressed (or repeated) on the works of the mind are no longer founded upon direct and intimate contact with the work, except in a minute proportion. This particular kind of inflation then means, as everybody knows, that literary production becomes dangerously impoverished (one can no longer speak properly of literary production where there are no more than half-a-dozen readers) and at the same time that a risk is being taken on the future: that of a quite ruinous devaluation. (. . .)

(From *La Littérature à l'Estomac,* 1950)

The Experiences of Writers

MICHEL LEIRIS

(. . .) So I had been dreaming of bulls' horns. I was dissatisfied with being a mere writer. The matador who turns danger into an opportunity of shining more brilliantly than ever and most displays the quality of his style when he is most in danger – this is what impressed me, this is what I wanted to be. By means of an autobiography concerning a domain in which reserve is usually considered essential – a confession whose publication would be dangerous for me in that it would be compromising and, by exposing it, make my life more difficult – I intended to rid myself once and for all of certain constricting modes of description, and at the same time to describe myself with the utmost purity, as much for my own satisfaction as to dissipate any erroneous view that others may have of me. To achieve my complete deliverance through catharsis, this autobiography must take on a form capable of exalting me and of being understood by others as much as possible. I depended for this on a certain rigour in the writing and on the tragic light that would illuminate the whole story, even in the choice of symbols that I would use: Biblical and Classical figures, theatrical heroes and, of course, the toreador – psychological myths that forced themselves upon me by the revelatory value they had for me and which were, from the literary point of view, the principal themes, the devices whereby some apparent grandeur could invest a region where I knew there was none. (. . .) So I believed that if anything was at stake, if the bull's horn meant anything, it was not without a certain duplicity that I risked my life: on the one hand, giving in to my narcissistic tendencies again; on the other, trying to find in others not so much a judge as an accomplice. Moreover, the matador, who seems to risk all for all, watches his figure and depends on his technical knowledge to overcome danger.

But there is for the toreador a real danger of death, which can never be so for the artist, unless in some way external to his art (as during the German occupation, when the writing of clandestine literature certainly involved such danger, but only in the sense in which it was part of a much greater struggle, and, in fact, quite independently of the writing itself). Can I therefore maintain the comparison and regard as valid my introductory essay 'if there was no more than the shadow of a bull's horn in a work of literature'? Can the act of writing ever be, for the professional writer, a danger, which although not mortal is at least a positive one?

To write a book that would be an act, such was the aim that it seemed to me I should pursue when I wrote *L'Age d'Homme*. (. . .)

(From *De la Littérature considérée comme une Tauromachie*, 1946)

Literary Language and Spoken Language

RAYMOND QUENEAU

It might seem that there were more urgent and vital questions in France than that of the Defence of the French Language. Yet several newspapers and weekly magazines regularly devote one or more columns to the said defence. I do not consider this aim to be futile, but it seems to me that in general the enterprise is tainted with a defeatist spirit, for it is always from the point of view of the defensive that such a defence is made and this defence always consists of prohibitions. It is always a matter of keeping in order, preserving, mummifying. But the French language should be defended from the point of view of the offensive, if the term 'French language' can still be used – since the *Serment de Strasbourg* it has been applied to language that has become almost incomprehensible to us.

Philologists and linguists know perfectly well that written French (the language that is generally being 'defended') has no more than a distant connection with real French, the spoken language. There are a number of reasons why this discrepancy is not more obvious: the preservation of spelling, obligatory schooling, the automatism that obliges one to pass from one language to another on official, administrative or solemn occasions. But the change is a profound one. The vocabulary has altered imperceptibly, enriched above all by contemporary events, but it is the syntax of spoken French that is moving further and further away from the syntax of written French.

It is understandable that the powers that be should have always tried to hide this state of affairs. It is certainly not up to the teachers to bring about this revolution in language. What is strange is that this transformation should have escaped the attention of most writers, at least until very recently. They have sought originality in much more respectable, often metaphysical domains. But they have not seen that it is in the use of new materials that a new, vital, vigorous and true literature would emerge. The use of a language still untainted with the dust of grammarians and the marks of pedagogues would of itself create new ideas. In a recent article a young poet whom I respect declared that he was convinced that the language used by Racine, Voltaire, Châteaubriand, Anatole France and Paul Valéry contained within its substance all the possibilities open to language. This is the very thing I am doubtful of. It was the use of German that created Luther's existentialism and it was the use of the neo-French of the Renaissance which gave Rabelais and Montaigne their sense of freedom. A new language gives rise to new ideas and new thinkers need a new language. It is not a question of 'forging new parts for a new language', as the poet mentioned above accuses me of believing, but rather of giving a new form to something that will not flow into the twisted mould of a worn out grammar.

Modern French will only become a true and fruitful language when it is used by philosophers and, of course, scientists. I shall salute the first mathematician to write in this new language which is one of the few riches left to this country.

(From *Langage Littéraire et Langage Parlé*, 1950)

Presentation of Les Lettres Nouvelles

The revue *Les Lettres Nouvelles* wishes to serve literature before everything else. Crushed beneath the weight of ideologies and preconceived opinions, a weapon of propaganda or a means of escape, generally reduced to language that has nothing to say, literature is nevertheless something more than an aesthetic pastime, a more or less polished form of entertainment, or an inadmissible means to ends that are its ruin. To maintain the dignity of literature is a worthy enough aim for us.

It is founded upon certain simple principles:

Literature is expression. The expression of the man who writes – this much is self-evident – and, beyond that, it is the expression of all men who see themselves in him. The domain of men is both vast and particular. It contains both the social and ideological life and the individual forms of the sensibility. The latter may be monstrous or aberrational – it does not matter. All literature is licit from the moment it is established as a privileged means of communication, outside all moral, political, or even logical censorship. It is answerable to no criteria but its own.

Literature is creation. A product of the activity of certain men, it aims, through the medium of the written word, to influence and change other men. It is a disinterested activity and derives its value from its own freedom: it is equally scornful of establishing itself in museums and academies as it is to provide manifestoes for immediate action. It is by more subtle ways that it is transformed into thoughts, feelings, new patterns of behaviour, that it becomes life fusing with life.

Literature is art. That is to say, a form of expression linked to a technique. This technique may conceal all appearances, or proceed to all that is most expected of it; it can even become invisible; but its absence is the absence of literature itself.

If, for the best reasons in the world, one of these conditions disappears or is effaced, then it takes literature with it, leaving only its by-products. If, on the contrary, literature is created, it leads through art to life, which is not only the durable life of masterpieces, but also that world of thoughts, feelings, sensations and desires, in which each of us moves, blindly most of the time, until literature, which is at once consciousness and technique, provides the key.

It is untrue that in turbulent times like ours literature must lose its interest or importance, since it opposes all clouding of consciousness and has always, even in secret, been the instrument of our deepest and most serious thoughts.

We wish to give this instrument a better chance of being heard, leaving established reputations to their mutual admiration, stars and leaders to their quarrels and processions, but welcoming all those who have something to say and who try to say it as well as possible. It is enough that the simplest of their readers should be aware of the appropriateness of their means to their chosen end, in other words, their integrity.

No other criterion exists in France at the moment to defend and to illustrate a literature that must be, past, present and to come, a changing literature.

(From 'Présentation des *Lettres Nouvelles*', March 1953)

The Zero Point of Writing

ROLAND BARTHES

It is possible to discern in certain writers today the search for a neutral writing, for a style at point zero, for a kind of inert state of form. A comparison borrowed from linguists may make this new fact clearer: we know that certain linguists, like the Dane Viggo Brondal, establish between the two terminals of a polarity (singular-plural, past-present) the existence of a third terminal, the neutral or zero terminal: thus between the subjunctive and imperative moods, the indicative appears as an amodal form.

Mutatis mutandis, the style at point zero is basically an indicative style, or, if one prefers, an amodal style; it would be true to say that it is a journalist's style, if it were not that journalism has fairly generally adopted optative or imperative (that is, emotive) forms of thought. The new neutral style stands in the midst of all these shouts and judgements without participating in any of them; it is composed of their very absence; but this absence is total, it implies no refuge, no secret; it cannot be said therefore that it is an impassable style; it is rather an innocent style.

Thus in *L'Etranger*, for example, Camus obtained a style of absence which almost attained to an ideal absence of style, that philosopher's stone of present-day writers. Unfortunately, the creation of an absence of style is comparable to the paradox of the acrobat who produces pure repose between two oscillations; it cannot be produced in time; for the exercise of a language (and objectively literature is nothing other than language) is bound to produce automatisms, constants, themes, in which there is no innocence, since they indicate the return of myth, that is, of literature; from the moment the writer is truly himself, that is, exploits the particularity of his talent (which for him is the very form of perfection), literature conquers him again; he can no longer overcome it. If he ruthlessly resists the temptation of any emotive emphasis whatsoever, he will merely create, by this very effort itself, a new preciosity, that of concision. Can a writer of the calibre of Camus escape the Flaubertization of writing? Such are the tragic dimensions of the dilemma.

Sartre's attempt has been more circuitous; with his usual perspicacity, Sartre places his writing prior to (*prior to*, not beyond) any work (or non-work) on vocabulary; he gives words a primary power of description, which cancels the principle of effect, whether it derives from amplification or restraint. In this way an important element of traditional writing disappears: rhetoric itself, that is, essentially, the techniques of allusion which presuppose a kind of disjunction, or gap between thought and form, and therefore the existence of a certain dualism between writing as a phenomenon and thought as an essence. This leaves a writing that is simple, brutal perhaps, in the sense that it conceals no secret. Its absence of secret is a very new element in writing; and its first manifestation is certainly not to be sought in the writing of the realists, for there myth, the reference to a secret world, is constantly and emphatically present. Writers with no personal thematic, those who practise the zero degree of style, are extremely rare, and, to have an idea of what this means, reference must be made to the brief moment represented by Voltaire. Today the need for a universal language is as strong as it was then, but it cannot be presented in the same historical terms. The solutions of order (in the decorative sense) and anarchy in writing must also be rejected, for they are too tied historically to the principle of a gratuitous and therefore culpable literature. The desire to commit his work must have led Sartre to use a neutral, innocent-seeming style, which allowed his compromised mind full play without embarrassing himself further by an additional compromise with manner or style. Depriving himself both of richness and simplicity – which is also a result of art – Sartre retains only the indispensable quality of eloquence, tension, tempo, fluency, as Sainte-Beuve would say. It is incontestably a victory for Sartre that no one has ever said that he wrote well. But it is an uncertain victory, severely limited by the historical conditions of present-day literature, and threatened, like that of Camus, by the almost fatal exploitation of a writing that can be neutral only at the outset.

Another solution to this squaring of the circle formed by a literary work without literature, would be an absolutely 'natural' verbal transformation, taking nature to mean here perhaps no more than society; this would mean, as in the work of Queneau for example, throwing literature wide open to the irruption of spoken forms in the complete simplicity of a state of nature (and not as in realistic or popularist description, as can be seen by comparing the writing of a Céline with that of a Prévert). We should then arrive at that rhetorical revolution proclaimed and aborted by Hugo. It must not be forgotten that literary language is essentially anachronistic; it has the particularity almost of a dialect. A more complete revolution cannot therefore be conceived than to make this language historic. But the writers are divided on this: some, like Sartre and Camus, wish to attain universality by stripping language of everything that is conventional or pertains to the absolute; others, like Queneau and Prévert, in certain of their writings, get as near as possible to a genuinely spoken language, in its most concrete social nature; the first depend upon a kind of immediate norm of language; the second on its real diversity.

It remains to be seen whether the solution to these problems rests with the writers alone. Every writer opens in himself the trial of literature; but if he condemns it, he always grants it bail, which literature then uses to defeat him; he may create a free language, but it will come back to him as a fabricated one, for luxury is never innocent; and it is this language, made stale and hard by the immense weight of all the men who do not speak, that he must continue to use. There is therefore an *impasse* of style, and it is the *impasse* of society itself; the writers of today feel it: for them the search for a non-style, for a zero degree of writing, is in fact an anticipation of an absolutely homogeneous state of society; most of them know that there can be no universal language outside the concrete, and no longer mystical or nominal universality of the civil world. The question posed by these problems of writing is therefore finally this: can language be liberated before History?

(From *Le Degré Zéro de l'Ecriture,* 1947)

Literature and the Right to Death

MAURICE BLANCHOT

(. . .) I say: 'this woman'. Hölderlin, Mallarmé and, in general, all those whose poetry has as theme the essence of poetry have seen, in the act of naming, a wonderful, but disturbing phenomenon. The word gives me what it signifies, but first it eliminates it. In order to say 'this woman', I must in some way or other extract from her her reality of flesh and bones, render her absent, annihilate her. The word gives me the being, but it gives me it deprived of being. It is the absence of this being, its nothingness, what remains of it when it has lost being, that is, the simple fact that it is not. From this point of view, to speak is a strange occurrence. Hegel, in this the friend and neighbour of Hölderlin, in an earlier essay than *The Phenomenology,* wrote: 'The first act by which Adam made himself master of the animals was to impose a name upon them, that is to say, he annihilated them in their existence (*qua* existants).' Hegel means that from that moment, the cat ceased to be a uniquely real cat and became also an idea. The sense of the word exists therefore, as preface to all words, a kind of immense hecatomb, an earlier flood, plunging the whole of creation into one universal sea. God created beings, but man had to annihilate them. It is then that they took on a meaning for him, and he in turn created them anew out of the death in which they had disappeared; but instead of beings and, as we say, existants, there was now only Being, and man was condemned to being unable to approach anything or see anything except through the meaning that he was obliged to give birth to. He saw himself enclosed in light, and this light certainly could not end, for the end itself was light, since it is in their end that beings have their meaning, which is Being.

No doubt my writing kills nobody. Yet when I say 'this woman', death itself is announced and is already present in my language; my language means that this person, who is there, can now be detached from herself, subtracted from her existence and her presence and suddenly plunged into a nothingness of existence and presence; my language signifies essentially the possibility of this destruction; it is, at every moment, a resolute allusion to such an event. My language kills nobody. But if that woman were not at every moment of her life threatened by death, bound and united to death by a tie of essence, I could not accomplish this ideal negation, this deferred assassination that is my language.

It is therefore entirely true to say that when I speak, death speaks through me. My speech is a warning that death is, at this very moment, let loose in the world, that it has suddenly risen between me and the being I am addressing: it is between us like the distance that separates us, but this distance is also what prevents us from being separated, for it is the condition of all understanding. Only death allows me to seize what I want to grasp; it resides in words and gives them their meaning. Without death, everything would crumble into absurdity and nothingness.

From this situation various consequences ensue. It is clear that in me the power of speech is also tied to my absence of being. I name myself, and it is as if I pronounce my death sentence: I separate myself from myself, I am no longer either my presence or my reality, but an objective, impersonal presence, that of my name, which is beyond me and whose petrified immobility serves me in the office of a gravestone pressing down over the void. When I speak, I deny the existence of what I say, but I also deny the existence of the person who says it: my speech, if it reveals being in its inexistence, affirms from this revelation that it is made from the inexistence of him who makes it, of his ability to separate himself from himself, of being other than his being. That is why, to have a true language, the life that is to bear this language must have experienced its own nothingness, it must have 'trembled in the depths and everything that was fixed and stable in it must have been shaken'. Language begins only with the void; plenitude and certitude do not speak; everybody who speaks is defective in some essential way. Negation is tied to language. At first, I do not speak to say anything, but it is a nothing that demands to speak, nothing speaks, nothing finds its being in speech and the being of speech is nothing. This formula explains why the ideal of literature could be this: say nothing, speak and say nothing. This is not the dream of a nihilism de luxe. Language perceives that it owes its meaning, not to what exists, but to a distance between it and existence, and it suffers the temptation of keeping its distance, of wishing to attain negation in itself and of making everything out of nothing. If one speaks of things only by saying of them that by which they are nothing, then, indeed, the only hope of saying everything is to say nothing. (. . .)

(From 'La Littérature et le Droit à la Mort',
La Part du Feu, 1949)

Experiences of Literature

JEAN REVERZY

Very late, at a time when my life was moving into decline, I suddenly took to writing. Not a page, but pages, a book, books. It was something I had long kept at the back of my mind, hesitating to unburden myself: the weight of a pen was enough to break my wrist. And yet, one evening, overcoming my lassitude, I set to work.

Up till then writing had been an obligation: letters of congratulation or condolence, certificates, diaries. My graphic work, a mass of words placed one after another, was not literature; it was even the opposite. From now on, I wrote because I wanted to; at first a page a day, then more.

In beginning this freely practised exercise, I preferred not to know what my motives were: I was merely aware that it was a serious and painful act that strengthened a solitude and a freedom that I previously feared I was losing.

At the trial of the white page, however, it proved that I was capable of no more than idle scribblings. But I comforted myself by repeating that it would come in the end. I was prudent enough not to read over what I had written and, by wise precaution, as soon as a sentence was finished, I forgot it. But no one can speak to a void: not daring to dedicate my writings to myself, I addressed them to a reader of the future, so hypothetical that I had nothing to fear.

The trial lasted for months, and it was always as painful as on the first evening. I feared it would have no end. On certain days, I would write three pages in two hours; on others, I could produce no more than a dozen words in the same time. In both cases, when my work was done, I felt worn out. But I had the courage to re-read what I had written and even to correct it: in doing so, I learned that literary creation is the art of transforming stammerings into speech. . . . And this led to a first book, a second, poems, a journal. Emerging victorious from the test, since I had not given up, and ready to go on, I became curious about the reasons for my devotion. And I began, pen in hand, to watch myself at work.

I had imagined characters that I wished to describe. It was easy to make out their faces or interpret their gestures; but I had difficulty in hearing what they said, for they moved far off, in a background of my imagination, talking quietly among themselves. And when they came nearer, I became deaf. In fact, I was trying to translate my interior language into correct French: for they are two quite distinct languages. The word mumbled in the mind possesses ramifications and a life which are quite absent from the written word. Thought knows nothing of grammatical agreements, harmony, verbs; it is a noisy jumble of nouns. I concluded that each day I was making a translation into French; but I corrected myself by affirming that it was a translation *from* French. Finally, I suspended judgement, no longer knowing what my real language was.

Sometimes, at the end of a sentence, I experienced a new feeling: doubt. Not as to the literary value of the sentence, but about its identity with the emotion I wished to express. And for the first time I caught a glimpse of the danger of style, the artifice by which the interior language is projected, according to certain norms, on to the paper and which, by the spell it exercises over the author reading over his work, almost succeeds in making him forget what he set out to do: the chance patterns of words and their associations combine to express an emotion that the writer had not felt and which, not without surprise and joy, he discovers in re-reading. In the same way that a painter, losing control of his lines and colours, constructs a work whose brilliance excites him so much that he forgets that his painting has no resemblance to the nature he had taken as his model.

I realized that many feelings and emotions could be transcribed only by a travesty in which the written word, a distant relative of the same word of the interior language, lost its own value to the point of no longer existing. I tried symbol, allegory, anecdote and, handling them fairly easily, I thought myself less obtuse. If the symbolic form revealed to me, possessing the key to the enigma, only my falsified thought, to the hypothetical reader, now less innocuous than at the beginning, since when my work seemed to me to be readable, it expressed unambiguously what I had felt and wished to say.

Thus I started to describe a landscape – a plain – a perfectly flat area in which suburb and drab countryside merged into each other, polluted by its proximity to the town, and which for a long time had attracted me so much that I would go every evening and contemplate it. This was no easy task in view of the complexity of the suburban landscape, divided up by innumerable streets, bordered by reinforced concrete buildings or small, working-class houses whose charm is lost in the monotony of a single, dull image. In the end, I made use of symbol and of a new artifice: my poem was meant to be a succession of counter-truths. I began it like this:

I do not like this hill.

At once I noticed the agreement between the writing and the interior feeling formed by the secret of my lie: I did like the plain. This complex plain, with its blurred outlines, was treated with a similar care for falsification; I wanted it to be simple:

Above the rubble and the brushwood, like an image of China, it bears the light weight of a ruined dungeon and three pines planted on its summit.

The lie got deeper; the urban plain became a rural hill. Its working people, towards whom I had tender feelings of familiarity, became treacherous rustics:

Here I have nothing to fear from men. When I first came here I killed twelve of them, because they brushed against me as they passed. Now I don't have to say to them: Get out of the way! In the streets, when they see my hawk's head and my huge hands, they scatter like a flight of partridges.

I had no difficulty in writing this. The hypothetical reader, who was getting in my way in any case, had disappeared without my being at all tempted to call him back. From then on I wrote only for myself. My half-glimpsed truths – what I too now call my view of the world – were now my exclusive concern, even though they might appear to be written for readers whom I would not not know and who would not know me. My means of expression were submitted to conventions established in secret, with myself. Others, of course, would interpret and judge: it would provide a pleasant pastime for them. They would admire or criticize a fallacious image through a thick incomprehension that literature has not the power to penetrate.

The suburban plain had inspired me to write four pages; when the last word was written, I promptly forgot it: it would no longer be the object of my walks. For me everything had been said about what had attracted me to its waste lands and if, out of necessity, I had to cross it again, I would pass beside a smooth landscape of which my mind would not retain a single detail. The plain and the emotion to which each evening a moment of my life had been suspended were now dead: breaking with my convention of counter-truth, I had written as much at the end of my text.

I had made use of a clever trick, and I imagined that there must be many others, some much better. I continued to hope that I would discover them. Gradually, however, literature appeared to me under a different light: writers were merely men experienced in the tortuous game of writing, which allowed them to translate a truth that they felt very strongly and, by doing so, rid themselves of that feeling – a translation that the reader would retranslate as best he could. The writer would be said to have this much, or that much talent – this word had struck me alternately as being meaningless and odious. I knew that talent, that counterfeit currency of Letters, was no more than a present made by the reader to the author, who alone knew whether he had succeeded or failed.

And I was no longer ignorant of the reason for my efforts: writing was purely and simply an attempt to destroy something. An instinct of self-destruction had forced me to continue with a task that had long been a painful one; there had been good reasons for my apprehension and my lassitude. I now knew that the success of a sentence abolishes the thought that inspired it, and the same thing applies to the whole work of which the last word marks the end of a dissolution, eagerly awaited through a long period of apprenticeship. The last full-stop was not, in fact, a reward; beyond, physical life would go on: the conditional being, the creature of reflexes would survive the death of that other being, the true being, now annihilated, expressed, scattered over the pages.

I sometimes thought of the books I had read; their characters lived for me as if I had known them. But I was no longer the dupe of my illusion. Those characters were my work; I had reinvented them, in my own way, for my own pleasure. For me they were still living beings; for their inventors they had been dead. As I had forgotten the heroes of my stories, the writers had forgotten theirs; one remembers the deaths of others, not one's own.

So I was surprised by this desire for eternity felt by so many authors in the past. By what aberration did someone who little by little destroyed himself dream of one day reaching the 'human memories' of a world he could not enter? The man who had written the message, forgotten almost as soon as written, and who alone could interpret it, would be no more; there would therefore no longer be a message. This is the contradiction at the heart of the writer: he conceives his survival and imagines that once he is himself dead his work, emptied of its substance, disfigured, untranslatable, can subsist after him, after his double death, spiritual and material. The living man worked towards death, the dead man aspired to survival.

But what was the death of others to me? I was beginning to

know my own: it lay at the end of my long, patient wait. And already, strengthened by experience, speaking to a future author hesitating before his first sentence, I gave him my fraternal advice: 'If you want to write, learn to die.'

(From *Expériences de Littérature*, 1955)

The 'New Novel'

NATHALIE SARRAUTE

(. . .) According to all appearances, not only has the novelist practically ceased to believe in his characters, but the reader, too, is unable to believe in them; with the result that the characters, having lost the twofold support that the novelist's and the reader's faith afforded them, and which permitted them to stand upright with the burden of the entire story resting on their broad shoulders, may now be seen to vacillate and fall apart.

Since the happy days of Eugénie Grandet when, at the height of his power, the character occupied the place of honour between reader and novelist, the object of their common devotion, like the Saints between the donors in primitive paintings, he has continued to lose, one after the other, his attributes and prerogatives.

At that time he was richly endowed with every asset, the recipient of every attention; he lacked for nothing, from the silver buckles on his breeches to the veined wart on the end of his nose. Since then he has lost everything: his ancestors, his carefully built house, filled from cellar to garret with a variety of objects, down to the tinest gew-gaw; his sources of income and his estates; his clothes, his body, his face. Particularly, however, has he lost that most precious of all possessions, his personality – which belonged to him alone – and frequently, even his name.

Today, a constantly rising tide has been flooding us with literary works that still claim to be novels and in which a being devoid of outline, indefinable, intangible and invisible, an anonymous 'I', who is at once all and nothing, and who as often as not is but the reflection of the author himself, has usurped the role of the hero, occupying the place of honour. The other characters, being deprived of their own existence, are reduced to the status of visions, dreams, nightmares, illusions, reflections, quiddities or dependents of this all-powerful 'I' . . .

(This evolution) shows, on the part of both author and reader, an unusually sophisticated state of mind. For not only are they both wary of the character, but through him, they are wary of each other. He had been their meeting ground, the solid base from which they could take off in a common effort towards new experiments and new discoveries. He has now become the converging point of their mutual distrust, the devastated ground on which they confront each other. And if we examine his present situation, we are tempted to conclude that it furnishes a perfect illustration of Stendhal's statement that 'the genius of suspicion has appeared on the scene'. We have now entered upon an age of suspicion. (...)

. . . The sense of life to which, in the long run, all art harks back (the 'intensity of life' that undoubtedly, as Gide says, 'is what gives things their value'), has deserted these erstwhile promising forms and betaken itself elsewhere. By virtue of the ceaseless movement which tends to bring it ever nearer to the mobile point where, at a given moment, experiment and the peak of effort meet, it has broken through the earlier novel form and forsaken, one by one, all the old, useless accessories. Today, warts and waistcoats, characters and plots, may offer the most infinite variety without revealing anything other than a reality, the slightest particle of which we are familiar with already, from having been over and over it, in every direction. Instead of inciting the reader, as in Balzac's time, to attain to a truth whose conquest denotes hard-won struggle, all these accessories now appear to him to constitute but a dangerous concession to his inclination towards laziness – as well as to that of the author – or to his fear of change. The swiftest glance about him, the most fleeting contact, tells him more than all these external appearances, the sole aim of which is to give a semblance of likelihood to the characters. He has only to dip into the huge stock, which as a result of his own experience is constantly increasing, to compensate for what is lacking in these tiresome descriptions.

As regards the character, he realizes that it is nothing other than a crude label which he himself makes use of, without real conviction and by way of convenience, for the purpose of orienting, very approximately, his own behaviour. So he is wary of the abrupt, spectacular types of action that model the character with a few resounding whacks; he is also wary of plot, which winds itself around the character like wrappings, giving it, along with an appearance of cohesiveness and life, mummy-like stiffness. (. . .)

. . . What he has learned is a matter of such common knowledge that there is no need to go into it here. He has made the acquaintance of Joyce, Proust and Freud; the trickle, imperceptible from without, of the interior monologue; the infinitely profuse growth of the psychological world and the vast, as yet almost unexplored regions of the unconscious. He has watched the watertight partitions that used to separate the characters from one another, give way, and the hero become an arbitrary limitation, a conventional figure cut from the common woof that each of us contains in its entirety, and which captures and holds within its meshes the entire universe. Like the surgeon who eyes the exact spot on which his greatest effort is to be concentrated, isolating it from the rest of the sleeping body, he has been led to centre all his attention and curiosity on some new psychological state, forgetting meanwhile the motionless character, who serves as its chance prop. He has seen time cease to be the swift stream that carried the plot forward, and become a stagnant pool at the bottom of which a slow, subtle decomposition is in progress; he has seen our actions lose their usual motives and accepted meanings, he has witnessed the appearance of hitherto unknown sentiments and seen those that were most familiar change both in aspect and in name.

In fact, he has learned so much and learned it so well, that he has begun to doubt whether the novelist's artificially constructed object is capable of secreting the wealth of the real object. And since writers of the objective school insist that it is useless to attempt to reproduce the infinite complexity of life, and that it is up to the reader to draw on his own resources, using the instruments of investigation he already possesses to wrest its mystery from the impenetrable object they present to him, he prefers to confine his efforts to certainties, and goes in for facts.

The 'true fact' has indeed an indubitable advantage over the invented tale. To begin with, that of being true. This is the source of its strength of conviction and forcefulness, of its noble indifference to ridicule and bad taste, as also of a certain quiet daring, a certain off-handedness that allow it to break through the confining limitations in which a regard for likelihood imprisons the boldest of novelists, and to extend far afield, the frontiers of reality. It allows us to attain to unknown regions into which no writer would have dared venture and brings us, with one leap, to the edge of the 'abyss'. (. . .)

. . . It goes without saying that all these attitudes with regard to the novel are all the more familiar to the author who, being himself a reader, and often a very perceptive one, has also experienced them.

The result is that when he starts to tell a story and says to himself that he must make up his mind to write down for the mocking eyes of the reader, 'The Marquise went out at five o'clock', he hesitates, he hasn't the heart, he simply can't bring himself to do it.

And if, after taking his courage in hand, he decides not to give the Marquise the considerate attention demanded by tradition, but to write only of what interests him today, he realizes that the impersonal tone, which is so well adapted to the needs of the old-style novel, is not suitable for conveying the complex, tenuous states that he is attempting to portray; the fact being, that these states resemble certain phenomena of modern physics which are so delicate and minute that even a ray of light falling on them disturbs and deforms them. Consequently, whenever the novelist seeks to describe them without revealing his own presence, he seems to hear the reader, like a child whose mother is reading him his first story, stop and ask: 'Who said that?'

A story told in the first person satisfies the legitimate scruples of the author. In addition, it has the appearance, at least, of real experience and authenticity, which impresses the reader and dispels mistrust.

For nobody today is entirely misled by the convenient

procedure that consists, for the novelist, in parsimoniously apportioning bits of himself, which he invests with a certain likelihood by dividing them, necessarily somewhat at random (if they have been taken from a cross-section performed at a certain depth, they are identical with everyone) among his characters. By a process of decortication, the reader then removes these bits and places them, as in a game of Lotto, in corresponding compartments he has discovered in himself.

Today, everybody is well aware, without being told, that '*la Bovary c'est moi*'. And since the important thing now, rather than to extend indefinitely the list of literary types, is to show the co-existence of contradictory emotions and to reproduce as closely as possible the wealth and complexity of the world of the psyche, the writer, in all honesty, writes about himself.

(From *L'Ere du Soupçon*, 1956, translated by Maria Jolas and included in *Tropisms* and *The Age of Suspicion*, 1963)

A Path for the Future Novel

ALAIN ROBBE-GRILLET

At first sight it hardly seems reasonable to think that an entirely *new* literature might one day – now, for instance – be possible. There have been many attempts, during the last thirty or more years, to get the art of fiction out of its rut, but they have only, at best, resulted in isolated works. And – as we are often told – none of these works, whatever its interest, has won the support of a public comparable to that of the bourgeois novel. The only conception of the novel that is current today is, in fact, that of Balzac.

It would not even be difficult to go back as far as Madame de la Fayette. For even in those days the same sacrosanct psychological analysis constituted the basis of all prose: it presided over the conception of a book, the description of its characters and the development of its plot. Ever since, a 'good' novel has always been the study of a passion – or of conflicting passions, or of the the absence of passion – in a given environment. Most of our contemporary traditional novelists – those whom the consumers actually approve of, that is – could copy long passages from *The Princess of Cleves* or from *Old Goriot* without arousing the suspicions of the vast public that devours their products. They would merely need to alter an occasional figure of speech, break up a construction or two, given an indication of the particular character of each by a word here or there, a daring metaphor, a turn of phrase. . . . But they all admit, though they see nothing extraordinary about it, that the things that constitute their major preoccupations, as writers, date back several centuries.

Why, they say, be surprised? The material – the French language – has only undergone very slight modifications in the last three hundred years and, if society has gradually been transformed, if industrial techniques have made considerable progress, our mental civilization, on the contrary, has not really changed. Our way of life is based on practically the same habits and the same taboos, whether moral, dietary, religious, sexual, hygienic, domestic, etc. And finally, there is the human 'heart', which – as is well known – is eternal. Everything has been said, and we were born too late, etc., etc.

The risk of such rebuffs is even greater if we care to claim that this new literature is not only a future possibility but is actually being written now, and that in fulfilling its mission it will represent a more total revolution than that from which, formerly, romanticism or naturalism were born.

There is inevitably something ridiculous about such a promise: '*Now* things are going to change!' What will they do, to bring about this change? What will they be moving towards? And, above all, why now?

But the present-day art of the novel is greeted with such apathy – which is recorded and discussed by all critics – that one can hardly believe that this art can survive much longer without some radical change. The solution that occurs to many people is simple: such a change is impossible, and the art of the novel is dying. This is not so sure. History will tell, after a few decades, whether its various recorded fits and starts are the signs of its death agony or of its rebirth.

In any case, we should have no illusions as to the difficulties involved in an upheaval of this sort. They are considerable. The whole existing literary establishment (from the publisher down to the humblest reader, by way of the bookseller and the critic) cannot help fighting the unknown form that is trying to assert itself. For even those who are the most inclined to welcome the idea of a necessary transformation, even those who are positively prepared to recognize the value of an experiment, are nevertheless the heirs to a tradition. And a new form, unconsciously judged in terms of the time-honoured, established forms, will always appear to be more or less an absence of form. (. . .)

. . . The inarticulate new-born babe will always be thought a monster, even by people who are enthusiastic about experiment. There will be curiosity, some show of interest, and reservations about the future. Most of the sincere praise will be directed to the vestiges of the past, to all the bonds the work has not yet broken and which are desperately trying to drag it backwards.

For if the standards of the past are used to measure the present, they are also used to construct it. The writer himself, however much he craves independence, is part of a mental civilization and a literature which can only be those of the past. It is impossible for him to escape, from one day to the next, this tradition of which he is the issue. Sometimes, even, the elements he has tried hardest to combat seem, on the contrary, to blossom more vigorously than ever in the very work in which he thought he had dealt them a mortal blow. And he will be congratulated, of course, and with relief, on having cultivated them so zealously.

Thus the specialists of the novel (whether novelists, or critics, or over-assiduous readers) will no doubt be the ones who will have the greatest difficulty in getting themselves out of the rut.

Even the least conditioned observer can't manage to see the world around him with an unprejudiced eye. Let us make it quite clear before we go any further that we are not here concerned with that naïve preoccupation with objectivity which so amuses the analysts of the (subjective) soul. Objectivity, in the current meaning of the term – a completely impersonal way of looking at things – is only too obviously a chimera. But it is *liberty* which ought at least to be possible – but isn't, either. Cultural fringes (bits of psychology, ethics, metaphysics, etc.) are all the time being attached to things and making them seem less strange, more comprehensible, more reassuring. Sometimes the camouflage is total: a gesture is effaced from our minds and its place taken by the emotions that are supposed to have given rise to it; we remember a landscape as being 'austere', or 'calm', without being able to describe a single line of it, or any of its principle elements. Even if we immediately think: 'But that's literature,' we don't try to rebel. We are used to this literature (the word has become pejorative) functioning like a screen, made of pieces of differently coloured glass, which splits our field of perception up into small, easily assimilable squares.

And if something resists this systematic arrangement, if some element in the world breaks the glass without finding any place in the interpretative screen, we can still make use of the convenient category of the absurd, which will absorb this irritating remainder.

But the world is neither meaningful nor absurd. It quite simply *is*. And that, in any case, is what is most remarkable about it. And suddenly this obvious fact strikes us with a force against which we are powerless. At one stroke the whole wonderful structure collapses: by opening our eyes unexpectedly we have experienced once too often the shock of this obstinate reality whose resistance we had been claiming to have broken down. All around us, defying our pack of animistic or domesticating adjectives, things *are there*. Their surface is smooth, clear and intact, without false glamour, without transparency. The whole of our literature has not yet managed even to begin to penetrate them, to alter their slightest curve.

The vast number of filmed novels that encumber our screens enable us to relive this curious experience as often as we like. The cinema, which is also heir to the psychological and naturalistic tradition, in most cases merely aims at transposing a story into pictures: it simply tries to impose on the spectator, by means of some well-chosen scenes, the meaning that the more leisurely comments in the book have for the reader. But what is always happening is that the filmed story drags us out of our comfortable state of mind and into the world it shows us, and with a violence we would look for in vain in the corresponding written text, whether novel or scenario.

Everyone can perceive the nature of the change that has taken place. In the original novel the objects and gestures that support the plot disappear completely and leave room only for their meaning: the vacant chair was only an absence or an expectation, the hand placed on the shoulder was only a sign of sympathy, the bars on the window were only the impossibility of getting out.... But now we *see* the chair, the movement of the hand, the shape of the bars. Their meaning remains obvious, but instead of monopolizing our attention it seems just like one more attribute; one too many, even, because what reaches us, what persists in our memory, what appears as essential and incapable of being reduced to vague mental ideas, is the gestures *per se*, the objects, the movements and the shapes, to which the picture has restored at one stroke (and unintentionally) their *reality*.

It may seem odd that these fragments of basic reality, which the filmed story cannot help unwittingly offering us, should make such an impression on us when identical scenes in day to day life would not suffice to free us from our blindness. It seems, in fact, as if the conventions of photography (the two dimensions, the black and white, the frame, the difference in scale between the foreground and the background) all help to liberate us from our own conventions. The slightly unusual appearance of this reproduction-world reveals to us, at the same time, the *unusual* character of the world around us; it too is unusual in so far as it refuses to submit to our habitual ways of understanding and to our notions of order.

And so we should try to construct a solider, more immediate world to take the place of this universe of 'meanings' (psychological, social, functional meanings). So that the first impact of objects and gestures should be that of their *presence*, and that this presence should then continue to dominate, taking precedence over any explanatory theory which would attempt to imprison them in some system of reference, whether it be sentimental, sociological, Freudian, metaphysical, or any other.

In the construction of future novels, gestures and objects will be *there*, before they are *something*; and they will still be there afterwards, hard, unalterable, ever-present, and apparently quite indifferent to their own meaning, which meaning tries in vain to reduce them to the precarious role of utensils, to a temporary and shameful fabric which has form only by kind permission of a superior human truth that has chosen it as a means of self-expression, after which it immediately reconsigns this embarrassing auxiliary to oblivion.

But from now on, on the contrary, objects will gradually lose their instability and their secrets, they will forego their false mystery, and that suspect inner life that an essayist has called 'the romantic heart of things'. They will no longer be the vague reflection of the vague soul of the hero, the image of his torments, the shadow of his desires. Or rather, if it does still happen that things are used for a moment as a support for human passions, it will only be temporarily, and they will only be making a more or less derisive show of accepting the tyranny of meanings, the better to indicate how far they remain alien to man.

As for the characters in the novel, they will be able to contain a multiplicity of possible interpretations; they will be open to every sort of comment to suit every sort of prejudice, whether psychological, psychiatric, religious or political. People will soon perceive their indifference to these so-called riches. Whereas the traditional hero is always being got at, cornered, destroyed, by the author's suggested interpretations, for ever being pushed into an intangible and unstable *elsewhere*, which gets more and more vague and remote, the future hero will on the contrary remain *there*. While it will be the comments that remain elsewhere; when the hero's presence is indisputable they will seem useless, superfluous, and even dishonest.

The exhibits described in a thriller give us, paradoxically enough, a fairly accurate illustration of this situation. The various elements collected by the detectives – an object abandoned at the scene of a crime, a movement immobilized in a photograph, a phrase overheard by a witness – these would all seem at first sight to call for an explanation, to exist only as a function of their role in an affair which is beyond them. But now various hypotheses begin to be built: the examining magistrate tries to establish a logical and necessary connection between the things; you think everything is going to resolve itself into a trite collection of causes and effects, intentions and accidents.

But the plot starts to thicken alarmingly: witnesses contradict one another, the suspect multiplies his alibis, new factors crop up which had previously been overlooked. . . . And you have to keep coming back to the recorded evidence: the exact position of a piece of furniture, the shape and frequency of a fingerprint, a word written in a message. The impression grows on you that nothing else is *true*. Whether they conceal or reveal a mystery, these elements that defy all systems have only one serious, obvious quality – that of being *there*.

And that is how it is with the world around us. We thought we had come to terms with it by giving it a meaning, and the whole art of the novel, in particular, seemed dedicated to this task. But that was only an illusory simplification, and far from becoming clearer and nearer, all that was happening was that the world was gradually losing all its life in the process. Since its reality consists above all in its presence, what we have to do now, then, is to build a literature which takes this into account.

All this might well seem highly theoretical and illusory were it not for the fact that something actually *is* changing – changing completely, even, and probably, permanently – in our relationship with the universe. Which is why we have some inkling of the answer to that very ironical question: 'Why now?' There is, today, in fact, a new element separating us, and radically, this time, from Balzac, Gide, or Madame de La Fayette: this is the poverty of the old myths of 'depth'.

We know that all fiction used to be based on them, and on them alone. The role of the writer traditionally consisted in burrowing down into Nature, in excavating it, in order to reach its most intimate strata and finally bring to light some minute part of a disturbing secret. The writer descended into the chasm of human passions and sent up to the apparently tranquil world (that of the surface) victorious messages describing the mysteries he had touched with his fingers. And the sacred vertigo which then overwhelmed the reader, far from causing him any distress or nausea, on the contrary reassured him about his powers of domination over the world. There were abysses, it was true, but thanks to these valiant speleologists their depths could be sounded.

It is not surprising that, in these conditions, the literary phenomenon *par excellence* consisted in the global and unique adjective, which attempted to unite within itself all the internal qualities and all the hidden soul of things. The word thus functioned as an ambush into which the writer lured the universe and then delivered it into the hands of society.

The revolution that has taken place is commensurate: not only do we no longer consider the world as a possession, our private property, designed to suit our needs, and domesticable, but, what is more, we don't believe in these depths any more. While essentialist conceptions of man were facing their doom, and the idea of 'condition' henceforth replacing that of 'nature', the *surface* of things has stopped being the mask of their heart for us, a sentiment which served as a prelude to all the 'beyonds' of metaphysics.

It was thus the whole of literary language that had to change, that is already changing. It is clear that those people who are the most aware are daily experiencing a growing repugnance towards words of a visceral, analogical or incantatory character. Whereas the optical, descriptive adjective, the adjective that is content to measure, to situate, to limit, to define, is probably showing us the difficult way to a new art of the novel.

(From 'Une Voie pour le Roman Futur', 1956, *Pour un Nouveau Roman*, translated by Barbara Wright as *Towards a New Novel*, 1965)

The Novel as Exploration

MICHEL BUTOR

I

The novel is a particular form of narrative.

Narration is a phenomenon that extends far beyond the field of literature; it is one of the essential factors in our apprehension of reality. From the moment we understand words to our death, we are constantly surrounded by narrative descriptions, in the family, at school, in our own lives and in our reading.

For us, other people are not only what we have seen of them with our eyes, but what they have told us about themselves, or what others have told us about them; they are not only those we have seen, but also all those others have spoken about.

This is not only true of people, but also of things, places, for example, where I have not been but which have been described to me.

This narrative that surrounds us takes on the most varied forms, from family tradition or the accounts one gives over the dinner table of what one has done during the day, to journalistic information or a work of history. Each of these forms links us to a particular sector of reality.

All these true narratives have one thing in common: they are always, in principle, verifiable. I must always be able to check what someone has told me against information supplied by someone else, and so on indefinitely; otherwise, I am faced either with error or fiction.

Among all these accounts that go to make up very largely our everyday world there are probably some that have been deliberately invented. If narrated events are given characteristics which – let us avoid any pejorative undertone – distinguish them at once from all those that come within our normal experience, we are confronted with a literature of fantasy, myth, fairy-tale, etc. The novelist, on the contrary, presents normal, everyday events and tries to give them the greatest possible appearance of reality, even to the point of mystification (Defoe).

But the story the novelist tells us is unverifiable and, consequently, what he says about it must be enough in itself to give it this appearance of reality. . . . From the moment a writer places the word 'novel' on the cover of his book, he declares that it is vain to seek (any kind of) confirmation. (. . .)

. . . Whereas the true story can always draw upon the support of external evidence, the novel is obliged to create the very thing it is describing. This is why the novel is *par excellence* in the field of phenomenology, a place in which we can study the way reality appears to us or can appear to us; it is why the novel is the laboratory of narration.

II

Work on the form of the novel is therefore of major importance.

As true stories become public and historical they gradually become fixed, ordered and reduced according to certain principles (the same ones that now govern the 'traditional' novel, the novel that asks no questions). For primitive apprehension is substituted another, one incomparably less rich, that systematically eleminates certain aspects of reality; it gradually covers up real experience, passes itself off as real experience, thus resulting in a generalized mystification. The exploration of different novel forms reveals what is contingent in the form we are used to, unmasks it, delivers us from it, allows us to rediscover beyond this petrified form everything that it conceals or which it remains silent about, all that fundamental narrative that is the element in which we live our lives.

Moreover, it is obvious that form being a principle of choice (and style, in this respect, is an aspect of form, the way in which the detail of language is put together, the deciding factor in the choice of one word or phrase rather than another), new form will reveal in reality new things, new relations, in proportion as their internal coherence is more vigorous than that of other forms.

Inversely, different narrative forms correspond to different realities. The world in which we live is being rapidly transformed, The traditional techniques of narration are incapable of integrating the new relations that have emerged. The result is a perpetual *malaise*; we cannot order in our consciousness all the information that assails it because we lack adequate tools.

The search for new forms, in the novel, of which the power of integration is the most important, plays therefore a triple role in our consciousness of reality, that of denunciation, exploration and adaptation. The novelist who refuses to perform this task, who demands no special effort from the reader, who does not upset him in his habits, who does not force him back on himself, making him question his most cherished opinions, certainly enjoys an easier success, but he acts as an accomplice of that profound *malaise*, that night in which we are all struggling. He helps to stifle consciousness, making its reflexes even more inflexible and its awakening even more difficult. However generous his intentions may be, his work acts in the last resort as a poison.

The creation of new forms in the novel, far from being opposed to realism, as short-sighted critics have imagined, is the *sine qua non* of a more far-reaching realism.

III

But the relation of the novel to the reality around us cannot be reduced to the fact that what the novel describes is presented as an illusory fragment of that reality, an isolated, manageable fragment that can be studied at close quarters. The difference between the events described in the novel and those of life is not only that the latter are verifiable, whereas the former can only be reduced through the words that create them. They are also more interesting, more profitable than real events. The emergence of these fictions corresponds to a need, fulfils a function. Imaginary characters compensate for what is lacking in reality and, at the same time, throw light on reality. (. . .)

. . . This application of the novel to reality is extremely complex, and its 'realism', the fact that it presents itself as an illusory fragment of daily life, is no more than one particular aspect of it, one that sets it apart as a literary form.

I call the 'symbolism' of a novel the totality of the relations it describes with the reality in which we live. . . . The external symbolism of the novel tends to be reflected in an internal symbolism, certain parts playing in relation to the whole the same role as the whole in relation to reality.

IV

It is obvious that it is this general relation of the 'reality' described by the novel to the reality around us that determines what is often called its theme or subject, which appears as a response to a certain situation of the consciousness. But this theme, this subject cannot be separated from the way in which it is presented, from the form in which it is expressed. So a new situation, a new consciousness of what the novel is, of its relations with reality, of its status, calls for new forms either in language, style, technique, composition or structure. Inversely, the search for new forms, revealing new subjects, also reveals new relations.

At a certain degree of reflection, realism, formalism and symbolism in the novel appear to constitute an indissociable unity. (. . .)

. . . The result of this is that any real transformation of the novel form, any profitable exploration into this field, can only come about within a transformation of the very idea of the novel, which is evolving slowly but inevitably (all the great works of the twentieth century are there to support this) towards a new kind of poetry that is at once epic and didactic.

Within a transformation of the notion of what literature is, literature begins to appear not simply as a luxury or an entertainment, but in its essential role within society, as methodical experiment.

(From 'Le Roman comme Recherche', 1955,
in *Répertoire*, 1960)

*English Translations of Books mentioned**

Louis Aragon		
La Semaine Sainte	Holy Week	Hamish Hamilton
Honoré de Balzac		
Eugénie Grandet	Eugenie Grandet	Everyman Series Heath: Harrap
Père Goriot	Old Goriot	Everyman Series Penguin
Simone de Beauvoir		
Deuxième Sexe	The Second Sex	Jonathan Cape Four Square
La Force de l'Age	The Prime of Life	Weidenfeld & Nicolson
L'Invitée	She Came to Stay	Secker & Warburg
Les Mandarins	The Mandarins	Collins
Mémoires d'une jeune fille	Memoirs of a Dutiful Daughter	Andre Deutsch & Weidenfeld & Nicolson
Pour une Morale de l'Ambiguité	Ethics of Ambiguity	H. Jonas
Le Sang des Autres	Blood of Others	Penguin
Samuel Beckett		
Comment c'est	How it is	Calder
La Dernière Bande	All That Falls	Faber
En Attendant Godot	Waiting for Godot	Faber Samuel French
Molloy Malone meurt L'Innommable	Molloy Malone Dies The Unnameable	Calder

* This list is not comprehensive, as many of the books mentioned do not appear to have been translated, or are now out of print.

Murphy	Murphy	Calder
Oh les Beaux Jours!	Happy Days	Faber
Antoine Blondin		
Les Enfants du Bon Dieu	The Children of God	Arco Publications
Michel Butor		
Degrés	Degrees	Methuen
L'Emploi du Temps	Passing Time	Faber
La Modification	Second Thoughts	Faber
Albert Camus		
La Chute	The Fall	Hamish Hamilton
L'Envers et L'Endroit Noces	Lyrical and Critical	Hamish Hamilton
L'Etranger	The Outsider	Hamish Hamilton
L'Exil et le Royaume	Exile and the Kingdom	Penguin
L'Homme Révolté	The Rebel	Penguin
Le Mythe de Sisyphe	Myth of Sisyphus	Hamish Hamilton
La Peste	The Plague	Hamish Hamilton Penguin
Jean Cau		
Les Paroissiens	The Village	Elek Books
Pitié de Dieu	Mercy of God	Heinemann
Louis-Ferdinand Céline		
Guignol's Band	Guignol's Band	Vision Press
Voyage au bout de la Nuit	Journey to the End of the Night	Vision Press
Jean-Louis Curtis		
Les Justes Causes	The Side of Angels	Secker & Warburg
Marguerite Duras		
Un Barrage Contre le Pacifique	Sea of Troubles	Methuen
Dix Heures du Soir en Été	10.30 on a Summer Night	Calder & Boyars
L'Après-midi de M. Andesmas	The Afternoon of M. Andesmas	Calder & Boyars

Moderato Cantabile	Moderato Cantabile	Calder & Boyars
Les Petits Chevaux de Tarquinia	Little Horses of Tarquinia	Calder & Boyars
Le Square	The Square	Calder & Boyars

Madame de la Fayette

La Princesse de Clèves	Princess de Cleves	Cambridge Penguin

Gustave Flaubert

L'Education Sentimentale	Sentimental Education	Everyman Series Penguin
Madame Bovary	Madame Bovary	Collins Everyman Series Oxford Penguin
Salammbô	Salammbo	Everyman Series

Louis-René des Forêts

La Chambre des Enfants	The Children's Room	Calder & Boyars

Roger Martin du Gard

Jean Barois	Jean Barois	John Lane

Romain Gary

Les Couleurs du Jour	Colours of the Day	Michael Joseph
Le Grand Vestiaire	The Company of Men	Michael Joseph
Lady L	Lady L	Michael Joseph
Les Promesses de l'Aube	Promise at Dawn	Michael Joseph Four Square
Les Racines du Ciel	Roots of Heaven	Penguin

Pierre Gascar

Les Bêtes	Beasts and Men	Methuen
Le Fugitif	The Fugitive	Andre Deutsch
La Graine	The Seed	Andre Deutsch

Jean Genet

Le Balcon	The Balcony	Faber
Les Bonnes	The Maids	Faber
Miracle de la Rose	Miracle of the Rose	Anthony Blond
Les Nègres	The Blacks	Faber
Notre Dame des Fleurs	Our Lady of the Flowers	Anthony Blond
Pompes Funèbres	Funeral Rites	Anthony Blond

André Gide

Les Caves du Vatican	Vatican Cellars	Cassell
Les Faux-Monnayeurs	The Coiners	Cassell

Jean Giono

Le Hussard sur le Toit	The Hussar on the Roof	Museum Press

Julien Gracq

Un Beau Ténébreux	The Dark Stranger	Peter Owen
Au Chateau d'Argol	The Castle of Argol	Peter Owen

Cécil Saint-Laurent

Caroline Chérie	Caroline Cherie	Pan

André Malraux

L'Espoir	Days of Hope	Routledge

André Pieyre de Mandiargues

Le Lis de Mer	Girl beneath the Lion	Calder & Boyars
La Motocyclette	The Girl on the Motor-cycle	Calder & Boyars

Francois Mauriac

La Fin de la Nuit	The End of the Night (Therese)	Eyre & Spottiswoode

Albert Memmi

La Statue de Sel	The Pillar of Salt	Elek Books

Robert Merle

L'Île	The Island	Michael Joseph
La Mort est mon Métier	Death is my Trade	Andre Deutsch

Michel Mohrt		
La Prison Maritime	Mariners' Prison	Weidenfeld & Nicolson
Michel de Montaigne		
Essais	Essays	Penguin
	Selected Essays	Manchester U.P.
		van Nostrand
Roger Nimier		
Les Enfants Tristes	Children of Circumstance	MacGibbon & Kee
Le Hussard Bleu	The Blue Hussar	MacGibbon & Kee
Robert Pinget		
Baga	Baga	Calder & Boyars
Le Fiston	No Answer	Calder & Boyars
L'Inquisitoire	The Inquisitory	Calder & Boyars
Mahu ou le Matériau	Mahu	Calder & Boyars
Marcel Proust		
À la recherche du Temps Perdu	Remembrance of Things Past	Chatto & Windus
Raymond Queneau		
Exercices de Style	Exercises in Style	Gaberbocchus
Pierrot, Mon Ami	Pierrot	Lehmann
Zazie dans le Métro	Zazie	Bodley Head
Alain Robbe-Grillet		
Dans le Labyrinthe	In the Labyrinth	Calder & Boyars
La Jalousie	Jealousy	Calder & Boyars
Les Gommes	The Erasers	Calder & Boyars
Le Voyeur	Voyeur	Calder & Boyars
Pour un Nouveau Roman	Towards a New Novel	Calder & Boyars
Dominique Rolin		
Le Souffle	Pulse of Life	Alvin Redman
Jules Roy		
La Vallée Heureuse	Happy Valley	World Distributors

Françoise Sagan

Bonjour Tristesse	Bonjour Tristesse	J. Murray Penguin
Dans un Mois dans un An	Those Without Shadows	J. Murray Penguin
Un Certain Sourire	A Certain Smile	J. Murray

Antoine de Saint-Exupéry

Courrier Sud	Southern Mail	Harrison Smith
Pilote de Guerre	Night Flight to Arras	Heinemann Penguin
Terre des Hommes	Wind, Sand and Stars	Heinemann
Vol de Nuit	Night Flight	Appleton

Nathalie Sarraute

L'Ère du Soupcon	Age of Suspicion	Calder & Boyars
Tropismes	Tropisms	Calder & Boyars
Fruits d'Or	Golden Fruits	Calder & Boyars
Martereau	Martereau	Calder & Boyars
Le Planétarium	Planetarium	Calder & Boyars
Portrait d'un Inconnu	Portrait of Man Unknown	Calder & Boyars

Jean-Paul Sartre

L'Être et le Néant	Being and Nothingness	Methuen
Les Chemins de la Liberté:		
1. L'Age de Raison	Age of Reason	Hamish Hamilton Penguin
2. Le Sursis	The Reprieve	Hamish Hamilton Penguin
3. La Mort dans l'Ame	Iron in the Soul	Hamish Hamilton
La Nausée	Nausea	Hamish Hamilton Penguin
Qu'est-ce que la littérature?	What is literature?	Methuen
Saint Genet, Comédien et Martyr	Saint Genet	W. H. Allen

Ignazio Silone

Fontamara	Fontamara	Jonathan Cape

Claude Simon

Gulliver	Gulliver	Jonathan Cape
L'Herbe	The Grass	Jonathan Cape

Le Palace	The Palace	Jonathan Cape
La Route des Flandres	Flanders Road	Jonathan Cape

Roger Vailland

La Fête	The Sovereigns	Jonathan Cape
La Loi	The Law	Jonathan Cape
Les Mauvais Coups	Turn of the Wheel	Jonathan Cape

Marguerite Yourcenar

Mémoires d'Hadrien	Memoirs of Hadrian	Secker & Warburg

Index